REVERBERATIONS FROM FUKUSHIMA

REVERBERATIONS FROM FUKUSHIMA

50 Japanese Poets Speak Out

Edited by

Leah Stenson and Asao Sarukawa Aroldi

INKWATER PRESS
PORTLAND • OREGON
INKWATERPRESS.COM

Cover and interior design by Masha Shubin, Japanese typography by Coal Sack Publishing Company.

Japan Flag Shaped From Origami Birds © Feoris. BigStockPhoto.com

Contact Inkwater Press at 6750 SW Franklin Street, Suite A, Portland, OR 97223-2542. 503.968.6777

Publisher: Inkwater Press | www.inkwaterpress.com

Reverberations from Fukushima : 50 Japanese poets speak out
/ edited by Leah Stenson and Asao Sarukawa Aroldi.
pages cm
LCCN 2013919161
ISBN 978-1-62901-065-6 (pbk.)
ISBN 978-1-62901-066-3 (epub)
ISBN 978-1-62901-067-0 (Kindle)

1. Japanese poetry. 2. Fukushima Nuclear Disaster, Japan, 2011--Poetry. 3. Nuclear energy--Poetry. 4. Nuclear power plants--Accidents--Japan--Poetry. Stenson, Leah. II. Aroldi, Asao Sarukawa. III. Title: Based on (work): Datsu genpatsu, shizen enerugī 218-nin shishū.

PL757.5.E32V65 2014 895.61'6080355
QBI14-600021

Paperback ISBN-13 978-1-62901-065-6 | ISBN-10 1-62901-065-0
Kindle ISBN-13 978-1-62901-066-3 | ISBN-10 1-62901-066-9
ePub ISBN-13 978-1-62901-067-0 | ISBN-10 1-62901-067-7

Printed in the U.S.A.
All paper is acid free and meets all ANSI standards for archival quality paper.

1 3 5 7 9 10 8 6 4 2

TABLE OF CONTENTS

Note: Pagination for the Japanese language section of this book begins from the 'back' cover, according to Japanese convention.

ACKNOWLEDGEMENTS

In addition to the Japanese publisher, editors, poets and translators who made this book possible, I wish to offer my deep appreciation to David Krieger, poet and founder of the Nuclear Age Peace Foundation, and nuclear policy expert Francesca Giovannini, whose contributions to this book will help us understand nuclear power in a broader context.

I also wish to extend special thanks to John Sibley Williams, my friend and fellow poet, who shared my enthusiasm for this project and connected me with Inkwater Press, and to Joan Maiers who provided thoughtful editorial advice.

I could have never undertaken this project without the support of my husband Bill who believes as deeply as I do in the importance of this book and has supported me on every step of this incredible journey from idea to publication.

And last but not least, I'd also like to extend my deep appreciation to everyone in both the US and Japan who gave me words of encouragement and to everyone who has expressed a willingness to help spread the poetry in this anthology far and wide.

Leah Stenson

REMARKS ABOUT EDITING THE TRANSLATIONS IN *REVERBERATIONS FROM FUKUSHIMA*

The poems in *Reverberations from Fukushima: 50 Japanese Poets Speak Out* were originally translated by native Japanese translators living in Japan, and the translations appeared in *Farewell to Nuclear, Welcome to Renewable Energy: A Collection of Poems by 218 Poets* published by Coal Sack Publishing Company.

In preparing the abridged anthology for publication in the United States, I felt it necessary to edit the original translations so as to make them more accessible to an American audience. Editing these translations was a challenge since I wanted to remain true to the poets' language and intended meaning while enhancing the readability of the poems and clarifying concepts and aspects of culture that might be unfamiliar to American readers.

A comparison of the poems will reveal a divergence between the translations published by Coal Sack Publishing Company and the 'translations' as they appear in the American anthology published by Ink Water Press. Despite having lived in Japan for 16 years and feeling at home in the culture and the language, I would never claim for myself the mantle of translator. Rather, viewing my role as that of an editor whose task it is to illuminate the translations, I have credited the original translators of the poems on each page of the English text.

For a list of the poems and page numbers as they appeared in Coal Sack's *Farewell to Nuclear, Welcome to Renewable Energy* please see "Page References for the Poems."

LEAH STENSON

PREFACE

Together with the rest of the world, I watched in horror and disbelief as the catastrophe of Fukushima played out before me like a Greek tragedy. Living in the American northwest about 200 miles downstream from the Hanford Nuclear Reservation, the highly contaminated site where plutonium was processed for the bomb dropped on Nagasaki, I was already concerned about radioactive contamination. Watching events unfold at Fukushima, I was acutely aware that I was only days away from an airborne radiation plume. I literally had a front row seat to the tragedy.

Over the next two years, as Fukushima dropped out of the 24-hour news cycle and receded from public consciousness, the American public remained largely unaware of the human toll of the tragedy. As we approach the third anniversary of the disaster, I've chosen to revisit the tragedy of Fukushima through Japanese voices that address the dark secrets and tragic impact of uranium-based nuclear power.

My hope in publishing *Reverberations from Fukushima: 50 Japanese Poets Speak Out* is two-fold. I want to open the eyes of the American public to the dangers inherent in uranium-based nuclear power, a technology as perilous as it is powerful. I also hope to enhance Americans' knowledge of contemporary Japanese poetry. Other than traditional haiku and tanka forms, Americans have had limited exposure to contemporary Japanese poetry. Hopefully, the selections presented in this anthology will increase their appreciation.

Living in the US, I faced the difficulty of finding poems. I was fortunate to make the acquaintance of my co-editor, Asao Sarukawa Aroldi, who joined the anti-nuclear movement in Japan following the disaster at Fukushima and served as a volunteer interpreter at anti-nuclear conferences. She undertook the difficult task of tracking down Japanese poets who had written on Fukushima. When she discovered *Farewell to Nuclear, Welcome to Renewable Energy: A Collection of Poems by 218 Poets*, edited by Hisao Suzuki, et.al. (Coal Sack Publishing Company, 2012), we sought permission from the publisher, who readily and most kindly allowed us to tailor *Farewell to Nuclear* to an American audience.

The result is *Reverberations from Fukushima: 50 Japanese Poets Speak Out*, published by Inkwater Press. This anthology is more than an outcry in response to the tragedy brought about by the nuclear accident. The fifty poets whose work is presented here speak for the thousands, millions, whose voices have not been heard, and they speak with eloquence, passion and courage.

The poems plead for restoration of balance between humans and the environment; provide eloquent testimony to the consequences of breaking with tradition and the cycle of life; present prophetic visions of a nuclear future that has sadly come to pass; lament the loss of home and livelihood; portray the exploited and the exploiters of human life bound together in a hellish cycle of destruction; unveil the lies fed to the Japanese public and decry how the nation was "brainwashed" into accepting nuclear power. Hopefully, putting a human face on the nuclear disaster through poetry will help American readers connect heart-to-heart with the people of Japan who suffered the terrible effects of Fukushima.

I feel very fortunate to have had the opportunity to meet Hisao Suzuki, the founder of Coal Sack Publishing Company, who not only gave me permission to republish the poems that appear in *Reverberations from Fukushima* but also introduced me to two poets from Fukushima Prefecture whose poems are included in this anthology. One is Masayuki Nemoto, a nuclear refugee who, in his poem "My Home, Namiemachi," memorializes the town he loved so dearly and was forced to abandon. It was he who arranged for me to enter the exclusion zone with my husband, who documented the trip, and my daughter, who served as an interpreter.

Visiting the deserted towns and countryside around the Daiichi Nuclear Plant served to give me a clearer understanding of the situation in the exclusion zone. Despite this experience, it is still difficult for me to grasp the scope and extent of the tragedy. Several hundred square miles of Fukushima prefecture are currently uninhabitable and nearly 150,000 people have been displaced and are living as nuclear refugees, many of whom may never return home. The so-called ghost towns, which included areas undamaged by the earthquake or tsunami, were like movie sets after all the actors had left and gone home. The complete absence of human activity in the context of shops, homes, and streets was eerie beyond description.

I also had the good fortune to meet Jotaro Wakamatsu, a poet and activist who lives in Minami-soma, an area bordering the nuclear exclusion zone. For decades he fought in the courts against locating the Daini Nuclear Plant in Fukushima. For his efforts to expose the dangers of nuclear power, he was ostracized by his neighbors who welcomed the revenue a nuclear plant would generate. Following the accident at Chernobyl, Mr. Wakamatsu visited the region and wrote the powerful poem, "A Land of Sorrow: A City Spirited Away By God, A Litany (6)" which is included in this anthology. This poem presciently foreshadowed the nuclear accident in Fukushima. However, instead of heeding his prophetic words, people derided Mr. Wakamatsu and Coal Sack founder Hisao Suzuki, his comrade in the battle against nuclear power, as "the boys who cried wolf."

I am honored to have met these three poets and am inspired by their tireless efforts to warn the world of the dangers of nuclear power. I am also gratified to know they found some solace in my effort to publish this anthology of poetry in the United States. Many of the residents in Fukushima feel forgotten, abandoned by their government, and the fact that their voices can now be heard outside Japan is a source of encouragement.

I owe a special debt of gratitude to Mr. Suzuki for connecting me to these poets and for supporting me in my effort to publish this anthology. In addition to being a publisher, Mr. Suzuki is also a fine poet whose poem "A Letter from the Shroud" is the lead poem in this anthology. We all owe a debt of gratitude to Mr. Suzuki for his social consciousness and steadfast determination to publish books that criticize nuclear power and decry the use of nuclear weapons.

The bond of solidarity and friendship I formed with the poets in Fukushima makes the publication of this book all the more meaningful for me. I'm firmly convinced that the more we unite for the good of humanity within our respective communities and countries, the better chance we will have at creating a safe nuclear-free world.

We all live under the same cloud, downstream from the plume. The simple truth is that nuclear accidents can wreak incalculable damage and we are only one black swan event away from another Fukushima—in my country or somewhere else in the world. Buddhist wisdom states, *"The cart that overturns on the road ahead is a warning to the one behind."* The question is whether we will learn from Fukushima–whether we will let the voices of these poets who speak the painful truth reverberate in our hearts and minds.

LEAH STENSON
PORTLAND, OREGON

Commentary

ON THE PUBLICATION OF THE AMERICAN EDITION OF *REVERBERATIONS FROM FUKUSHIMA: 50 JAPANESE POETS SPEAK OUT*

By Jotaro Wakamatsu

It seems to me important to begin by providing a summary of the situation in Fukushima as of this volume's publication.

Operations to remove the spent fuel rods from reactor 4 at Fukushima Daiichi got underway in November 2013. Although some two years and eight months have passed since the nuclear disaster, there has yet to be any precise confirmation of the status of reactors 1 through 3 where meltdowns occurred. Despite severe deterioration of the nuclear power plant building and of plant maintenance equipment due to damage resulting from the hydrogen explosions and the high temperatures produced by the nuclear fuel, only makeshift measures have been possible. Large quantities of radioactive materials continue to be released into the air and water; the situation is such that anything could happen at any time. In view of the experience at Chernobyl, we may surmise that resolving the critical conditions at Fukushima to the point of the reactors being decommissioned will likely require longer than a human lifetime to complete.

In April 2013 the evacuation zone was divided into three zones based on the quantity of radiation. Barriers prohibiting entry and roadblocks were then newly erected at more than 570 locations in Futaba District.

More than 140,000 people have been driven from the place of their daily lives; even now, as we approach the three-year anniversary of the nuclear disaster, they remain compelled to lead lives of deprivation through no fault of their own. In addition, there are many others who, for lack of any alternative, continue living in areas with radiation levels high enough to justify their evacuation. How long will this state of affairs in which people are effectively abandoned be permitted to continue?

I live in Minamisoma, a town 25 kilometers from Tokyo Electric's Fukushima Daiichi, the power plant that produced the nuclear disaster that has horrified people the world over. At the time I took up residence in this town in 1962, there were not yet any nuclear power plants in Japan. When reactor 1 of Tokyo Electric's Fukushima Daiichi—the fourth nuclear reactor in Japan—commenced operations in 1971, I had the opportunity to tour the facility and write an article about the power plant. I came to hold a critical view at that time, harboring simple doubts as to why such a facility should be built in a rural area so far away from the place where the power would actually be consumed; it was almost as if the plant were purposely being hidden from view. In 1975, I was one of 404 plaintiffs who filed suit against the government in Fukushima District Court demanding that permission for the establishment of reactor 1 at Fukushima Daini power plant be rescinded. In the aftermath of the nuclear disaster, I have been actively involved in Plaintiffs Against the Fukushima Nuclear Plant and submitted letters of complaint.

War is a crime of the utmost gravity because not only does it rob people of their lives, it also robs people of their homeland and way of life. As a society, we have become lax in pursuing responsibility for war crimes. As a consequence, we Japanese still find ourselves in a situation, in which no one has truly taken the responsibility for those war crimes. A nuclear disaster is similarly also a crime of the utmost gravity because it robs people of their lives, their homeland and their way of life. If culpability for this crime is glossed over and we entrust the cleanup of the nuclear disaster to later generations, and subject those generations to the dangers of additional radiation exposure, then we will have to hang our heads in shame before our posterity. On the contrary, we must endeavor by every means possible to ensure that no harm comes to the lives of youth, of children, and of those yet to be born.

If it is true that one of the roles of poetry is to censure the age, then surely poets ought to use words to focus a critical light on this situation. Through poetry it ought to be possible to translate the local problems of areas with nuclear power plants into universal problems faced by people everywhere.

Of the authors whose works are included in this volume, five are residents of Fukushima Prefecture—Masayuki Nemoto, Hiroshi Suzuki, Takao Ota, Tamiko Kido, Jotaro Wakamatsu. Three were born in Fukushima Prefecture—Setsuko Okubo, Chihiro Uozumi, Shonai Haga, and one—Makoto Yoshida, is deceased.

The legal challenge mentioned above demanding revocation of the permit for reactor 1 at Fukushima Daini power plant was dismissed by the Fukushima District Court in 1984. At that time, Makoto Yoshida (1933–1987) of Iwaki composed "Heavy Days and Years," eloquently articulating the issue at the heart of the problem with nuclear power.

Someday nuclear power
will certainly turn its fangs on people.

. . . .

To forever reject this monster—
therein lies our raison d'etre.

. . . .

If we should be negligent in this
then surely our grandchildren will someday ask:
"What did your generation do?"

In addition to "Toward a New Spring," which treats the radiation exposures of nuclear plant workers, his works also include "Message" and "On the Chernobyl Nuclear Power Plant Accident."

Masayuki Nemoto, who resided in Namiemachi which was heavily irradiated, even now, three years later, continues living as a refugee in Soma. In the poem "My Home Namiemachi," he describes his feelings on having been driven from the place he grew up and having lost his familiar way of life. Tamiko Kido's "Fairyland," Setsuko Okubo's "To My Home" and Chihiro Uozumi's "The Place Where the Soul Flies" are each infused with poignant sentiments on the loss of one's home through the experiential lens and words of each author. In "Decontamination," Hiroshi Suzuki exposes the fraudulent practices of nuclear clean-up firms that profit from the disaster while merely pretending to dispose of radiation:

They eliminate the surface soil and wash the walls and roofs.
That is the disguise called decontamination.
Where can we flush away things
that will never become clean
in twenty thousand years?

In "Life Is a True Treasure," Takao Ota expresses chagrin at having been deceived by the fiction of "peaceful utilization" and the "myth of security" of nuclear power while turning his thoughts to the children. In "Fetal Activity of Blue," Shonai Haga stakes his hopes on pregnant women who, in times of life-threatening danger, internalize the blue of heaven and the sea and nurture it as a fetus.

I would also like to introduce a number of Fukushima poets whose works are not included in this volume.

To the best of my knowledge, among the poets residing in Fukushima Prefecture, the first to express fear of nuclear power plants in a poem was Namiko Amagi (1915-2001) of Fukushima City who gave a reading of the poem "Burning Mirage" during a visit to Fukushima Daiichi in 1978. She writes:

A mirage rushing toward a world of decay
beyond the breeder reactors No. 5, No. 6,
I glimpse
a bird's-eye view of desolation 50 years hence.

Well before 50 years passed, we have already come to catastrophe. Her writings include a message of sympathy to the anti-nuclear power movement in Horonobe, Hokkaido, titled "Greetings to Horonobe" (1985).

There are a number of poets who worked at the nuclear power plant. In such highly realistic works as "Nuclear Power Plant" and "Nuclear Plant Inspection," Osamu Kon, who lives in Minamisoma, describes his first-hand experience of oppressive conditions as a laborer from the late 1980's through the early 1990's at Fukushima Daini, Hamaoka, Kashiwazaki-Kariwa and other plants. In one place, he writes, "I swam through highly concentrated radiation."

Naked comrades bump into one another
and change into work clothes of the same color.
Hundreds, thousands...
faces disappear, names disappear.
They become one person.
Everything is done based on registration number.
During the sweat-drenched work,
the fingers become wrinkled inside rubber gloves.
The full-face masks seal in the sweat,
The work clothes are like a damp mop.
Sweat that flows into the eyes, into the mouth,
tastes different in the morning from the afternoon.
. . . .
The people within
the hated and opposed nuclear power plant
labor under a shadow even darker than that of prisoners.
Extinguishing volition, neither opposing nor affirming anything,
they silently carry out their work within the set parameters.

(from "Nuclear Power Plant")

In "The Ocean, Now" (2000), Katsuo Sasaki of Minamisoma questions his own will to live:

People,
seeking convenience and spurring the consumption of electricity,
seek to increase the number of nuclear power plants on the coast.

. . . .

The sea now
asks if it is right or wrong to do so,
beckoning us to "understand what it is to have enough."

. . . .

People's hearts are bewildered,
and in bewilderment we are carried along.
As if the ground to stand on is slipping away,
we fail even to seriously discuss what will become
of the uranium and other materials used as fuel.

Sasaki, having lost his home, now lives in temporary housing in the city.

Hiroko Miura's poems include "See You Later," describing a nuclear plant worker who absconds, and "Day of News" (2001), chronicling a day in the removal of spent nuclear fuel from the reactor. Miura fled Namiemachi, which is adjacent to the Fukushima plant, and presently lives, by necessity, as a refugee in Soma. Kazunari Sato, who in 2011 wrote "Night," which describes the anxiety of a town with a nuclear power plant, moved from Tomiokacho to Koriyama and continues to lead the life of an evacuee.

The predictions that Masuo Hakozaki (Iwaki, 1914-1988) made in "Bird of the Sun" have now come to pass:

There is a thermal mass that would completely consume the world until the final moment.
For that reason, it is hermetically sealed
to ensure that it does not leak out,
that it is not exposed.
As long as it remains sealed,
"safety" must be emphasized.
That is, victory is emphasized
from the start of the war until the end—
sometimes with the solemnity of casting spells to sanctify
the gohei* *of "kamikaze,"*
sometimes with empty ritual, at times of collapse
when these are understood to be lies.

(from "Bird of the Sun")

I also want to touch on a number of works by poets from outside of Fukushima Prefecture that are included in this collection.

Fumiko Suzuki's "On the Night Marking Summer's End" (1987)

* Zigzagging paper streamers used as ceremonial ornaments in Shinto rituals.

criticizes the problem of workers being exploited and then abandoned once they have suffered radiation exposure under slip-shod working conditions. Mariko Fukuda's "Site Where Dangerous Objects Are Buried" discusses the problem of contaminated waste at Chernobyl. And Yukari Mutou's "Fresh Air" voices concern about the radioactive materials that are inevitably dispersed whenever an accident occurs.

In "Helen Keller's Fingertips," Masanori Shida says:

Helen Keller, on a return trip to Japan in 1948,
visited Hiroshima.
She directly touched the A-bomb survivors' keloid scars
and came to understand the horrors of the Atomic Bomb.

In contrast to us who "cannot see, though we have eyes [and] cannot hear, though we have ears," she imagines the following scene:

If Helen were to visit Fukushima now
and touch the ground with her fingertips,
what kind of scream would pierce her skin
and shake her soul?

In "Church Rock & Fukushima," Itsuko Ishikawa, conjuring images of an old woman of the Navajo tribe and an old woman exposed to radiation at Fukushima, presents the issues of discrimination and of people abandoned by the state. Hatsuko Hara's "The Day My Professional Career Ended" may be viewed as an instance of whistle-blowing by a former employee of the Tokyo Electric Power Company who resigned five months after the accident. Shouji Mitsui's "A Different Version of 'A Record of the Living'" describes the plight of animals that people left behind and criticizes the irony of slogans such as "A rich life with a proper understanding of nuclear energy" and "The development of an atomic town and a prosperous future" that adorn the welcoming archways to the village of Futaba.

Faced with the specter of a "nuclear disaster" that we ourselves had raised, we were compelled to think in terms of long periods of time. Kazuko Shimomura's "Let's Listen to the Voiceless Voice" offers observations against the yardstick of the 7,000-year lifespan of the Jomon cedar. In "Our Housedog Was Watching Us," Akira Kijima speaks in terms of "a thousand years, or . . . ten thousand years." And Keiichiro Fujitani, in "The Swindling of One Million Years," laments:

For the sake of your prosperity
of the next several decades,

haven't you swindled one million years
from the Japanese archipelago?

Not only have people irreverently invaded the domain of the gods and created radioactive materials not existing in the natural world, but, lacking the power of imagination toward life, they put these materials to mistaken and improper use. In the first place, the operation of nuclear power plants in the Japanese archipelago, which is situated over a seismic belt, is a problem in itself. Whether or not one lives in an area where a nuclear plant is located, one is certain to be impacted by a new March 11, 2011 brought to life by the restarting of more than 50 nuclear plants throughout the country.

What can we do for the sake of those who will be born in the future? That is the impulse behind Akito Kitahara's words in "The Heartbeat."

I am confident that if Japan's prime minister were a woman, after reading Jun Nakamura's "To the New Generations" and Rumiko Kora's "To Give Birth," there would be no approval given for the restarting of Kansai Electric Power Company's reactors 3 and 4 at Ooi, no exporting of nuclear power plants to other countries and, furthermore, no statements would be made about Tokyo being safe because contaminated water from the Fukushima Daiichi reactor was completely contained within a 300 square meter area in the harbor.

I would like to express my respect and gratitude to Ms. Leah Stenson for publishing this volume *Reverberations from Fukushima: 50 Japanese Poets Speak Out* in the United States. And I pray that many people in the English-speaking world will read this book and come to share a desire for the abolition of nuclear weapons and eradication of nuclear power.

MAKING THE WORLD AN "OPEN HOUSE"

Preface to *Reverberations from Fukushima: 50 Japanese Poets Speak Out,* the American edition of *Farewell to Nuclear, Welcome to Renewable Energy: A Collection of Poems by 218 Poets*

By Hisao Suzuki

I

Farewell to Nuclear, Welcome to Renewable Energy: A Collection of Poems by 218 Poets (combined Japanese-English edition, blurb and preface by Ryuichi Sakamoto), which was published on August 11, 2012—one year and five months after the Great East Japan Earthquake and the Tokyo Electric Power Company's Fukushima Daiichi Nuclear Power Station accident—elicited a broad response in Japan. The *Tokyo Shimbun* newspaper, which provided the most continuous coverage of the damage stemming from the nuclear power station accident of any major daily, ran a feature in which poems from the anthology were serialized. Due to strong positive reader response, the feature was extended from the initial plan of eight to 12 installments. An essay by the featured poet and a short biographical sketch complete with a photograph appeared alongside each poem. This was the first time ever that a Japanese newspaper had devoted so much space, and had serialized over such a long time, material from a poetry collection on a social topic. Dr. Asao Sarukawa Aroldi, an art historian who read the series, sent a copy of the poetry anthology to the poet and editor Leah Stenson, in Portland, Oregon, in the United States. Ms. Stenson, who lived in Japan for more than 16 years, had been searching for a suitable text through which to introduce American readers to poems by Japanese authors whose work addressed the experience of the Great East Japan Earthquake. In early 2013, Ms. Stenson sent me a letter translated by Dr. Sarukawa Aroldi, in which she outlined a basic proposal to select poems by 50 of the 218 poets to be published in the United States. Moved by the sincere desire of Ms. Stenson to make the plight of earthquake victims and those exposed to radiation known to a wider audience, I offered her my wholehearted support in this endeavor. I had published the combined Japanese-English edition out of a desire to convey to people throughout the world an understanding of the catastrophe of the great earthquake and nuclear accident. Gathering together the power of poets of Japan, I wanted to ensure that as many people as possible could learn from the experience of Fukushima. In deciding to go forward with this ambitious project, I felt that I would be able to rely on Ms. Stenson to lend her capable assistance to ensure that the message of *Farewell to Nuclear* could be spread to a wider audience. Dr. Sarukawa Aroldi visited Coal Sack on behalf of Ms. Stenson in September 2013, and in November Ms. Stenson, accompanied by her husband, visited us to discuss the translations and publication plan. At that meeting, I communicated to them Mr. Wakamatsu's and my expectations about editorial policy. In this way, the manuscript for the American edition was brought to near final form. As the person who had planned, edited and published the poetry collection that is the basis for this anthology, it has been a source of immense joy and satisfaction for me to see the American edition come to print in the short interval of less than one year. And for that I would like to express my heartfelt praise and gratitude for the passion and dedication demonstrated by Ms. Stenson who organized and edited this American edition.

I have long dedicated myself to composing poems and writing poetry critiques. In 1997 I accompanied Chisho Hamada, a poet whom I love and respect, to Hiroshima, where he delivered a speech at the invitation of the poets in that city. During his talk, Mr. Hamada urged Japanese poets to inscribe the pain of radiation victims in verse, even if they themselves had not suffered radiation exposure, and in this way they could broadcast the "Hiroshima philosophy" to the world—the tenet that what happened at Hiroshima and Nagasaki must never be allowed to occur again. Encouraged by Mr. Hamada's Hiroshima philosophy, which urges us to transcend enmity and the desire for revenge; and aspire to realize true peace through the abolition of nuclear weapons, some 10 years later I was able to publish *Against Nuclear Weapons: A Collection of Poems by 181 Poets* in (Japanese and English editions). Mr. Hamada, who applauded the book's release, passed away in 2008. Mr. Hamada had been a soldier in the Second World War and fought the American Forces in the Aleutian Islands and Kuril Islands. The sight of this man, who returned home having lost many comrades in arms, standing before the Atomic Bomb Dome and pledging to renounce war, and the awareness of how he steadfastly urged others to join him in composing poems calling for the elimination of nuclear weapons, will forever remain emblazoned in my heart. It would seem that my father's generation was the most tragic generation of the 20th century. I came up with the idea of undertaking a publishing project to collect poetry dealing with the tragedy of my father's generation and also encourage the writing of new poetry on the subject, in order to bequeath this legacy to future generations. Toward that end, in 2006 I established a publishing company; and to date I have published titles including: *Against Nuclear Weapons: A Collection of Poems by 181 Poets* (Japanese and English editions) (2007), *The Great Air Attacks: A Collection of Poems by 310 Poets* (2009) *Requiem: A Collection of Poems by 404 Poets* (2010), and *Lives in Danger: A Collection of Poems by 310 Poets* (2011). In the course of editing these volumes, it came to my attention that numerous anti-nuclear poems foreseeing an accident at a nuclear power station were being written. My parents were born in Fukushima Prefecture, and I myself had been writing poems about nuclear power stations for 20 some years. It thus came to pass that in the summer of 2012 I was able to publish the volume *Farewell to Nuclear, Welcome to Renewable Energy: A Collection of Poems by 218 Poets.*

II

Incidentally, from time to time I read from an anthology of works by my favorite American poet, Theodore Roethke, who resided in the state of Michigan. I am particularly fond of the title poem from his book *Open House* (1941). One feels as if the line in the second stanza *My truths are all foreknown, / This anguish self-revealed* anticipates the suffering of the coming catastrophe of the Second World War. The passage in the third stanza where he says,

> *The anger will endure,*
> *The deed will speak the truth*
> *In language strict and pure.*
> *I stop the lying mouth*

can be interpreted as expressing anger toward the bloated "lying mouth" that foments war in the name of the State. My mind is captured by this poem which conveys Roethke's ardent spirit to stand against the current of the age and solemnly protect "language strict and pure." The original English text is simple and conveys a startlingly noble spirit. I believe that Roethke was putting himself in the position of humankind when he composed this poem.

Of the Japanese poets of the 20th century, I wonder if even those commanding the greatest love and reverence among the Japanese are known to people in the United States. Most Japanese poetry fans would surely cite Kenji Miyazawa as one such poet. In his *Introduction to Farmers' Arts* Kenji writes, "No individual can be happy unless the whole world becomes happy." Putting his ideas into practice, Kenji composed thousands of pages of design drawings detailing fertilization of rice paddies. These were intended for farmers in the Tohoku region, which had experienced a succession of poor harvests. Kenji lived out his life as if carrying out a bodhisattva practice, and passed away in 1933 at the age of 38. Earlier, Japan had instigated the First Sino-Japanese War. In 1937, Japan began the indiscriminate bombing of Chinese cities and in 1941 attacked Pearl Harbor, bringing enormous tragedy to Asia and the Pacific. In direct contrast to Kenji's spirit, Japan's political and military leaders incited in the Japanese people the madness to invade Asia.

From this historical viewpoint, Japan must continue to bear its responsibility as a perpetrator of war crimes in the Sino-Japanese War and the Pacific War. I also believe that the conscience of American poets such as Roethke and the poets who have initiated and supported projects such as *Reverberations from Fukushima* will someday lead to the emergence of a world in which the Manhattan Project is reappraised, and where the wisdom exists to abolish nuclear weapons and nuclear power, its derivative technology.

III

Lastly, I would like to cite the opening of my commentary in *Farewell to Nuclear, Welcome to Renewable Energy: A Collection of Poems by 218 Poets*. This should provide readers with a good understanding of my reasons for having dedicated myself to publishing collections of socially conscious activist poetry.

> Poets are people who are sensitive to the coming and going of the seasons and the changes in nature. Their sharp power of observing nature is a power to foresee the crises and feel an anxiety for the future of humankind and Earth. Besides writing on their other individual subjects, many poets have written about their fears of nuclear weapons and nuclear power stations, which spread radiation over the entire natural environment of the Earth. We have asked not only Japanese poets, but also poets from other countries around the world to send their poems—both those which were written, with worries about the future, before the Great East Japan Earthquake of March 11 and those written after it occurred. The result is this anthology: *Farewell to Nuclear, Welcome to Renewable Energy: A Collection of Poems by 218 Poets*. It consists of 11 chapters. We have collected poems about denuclearization and have recorded the history of our activities for stopping nuclear energy. We still are dealing with the continuing disasters in Fukushima, and we feel we must carry out activities for denuclearization and put up a signpost for both the present and future, based on natural energy. The chapters are as follows:

We asked poets to send their poems to our poetry magazine, *Coal Sack,* and six editors–Hisao Suzuki, Jotaro Wakamatsu, Yorifumi Yaguchi, Fumiko Suzuki, Hiromi Mishou, and Kenichi Saso–recommended them and selected them. Seven bilingual poet-translators translated the poems. The translators are: Naoshi Koriyama, Yorifumi Yaguchi, Aya Yuhki, Junko Kimura, Keiko Shimada, Eriya Tanase, and Yuko Sawabe. When translations were made, native English-speaking readers also checked them, and in the case of non-English poets' poems, special language experts helped to make the translations.

The nuclear accidents at Tokyo Electric Power Company's Fukushima Daiichi Nuclear Power Station have exposed the grave problems concerning the field of nuclear power generation to the world. These accidents will go down in history as a crossroads that changed our thinking about the values of modern technology. The disaster, which has proven to be as serious as that of Chernobyl, profoundly shocked Germany, Italy and Switzerland, to the extent that these countries have sagaciously decided to close their nuclear plants. The United States discovered the method to produce fission of the nuclei of atoms in 1938 and seven years later, they dropped atomic bombs on Hiroshima and Nagasaki in 1945; and then, in 1954 in the South Pacific, they carried out tests using hydrogen bombs which were one thousand times as destructive as the Hiroshima-type bombs, contaminating the Lucky Dragon and more than 1,000 other fishing boats. The radioactive substances contaminated the entire Earth. In order to pass over the real facts of the hydrogen bomb tests at Bikini Atoll in silence, the United States proposed to provide its allies such as Japan with an derivative technique for producing electricity from a mini-type nuclear reactor, such as the ones used in submarines. The Japanese government knew well how seriously the radiation of the atomic bombs could afflict the survivors of the atomic-bombing, but it thought that the energy from nuclear power generation would be different from that produced by nuclear bombs. It used the impressive phrase "peaceful use of nuclear energy," and accepted the "devil's technology" of obtaining energy by splitting the nuclei of atoms. Japan had the responsibility to tell the entire world how terrible atomic radiation could be, but it did not take the responsibility it owed the entire world. Japan has chosen the way to become the perpetrator by contaminating the world with the nuclear disaster in Fukushima. Japan accepted its decisive defeat in the war, after the dropping of the atomic bombs. The recent nuclear disaster in Fukushima may well be called Japan's "second defeat." Its cause was brought about by underestimating the radiation of the hydrogen bomb test at Bikini Atoll and by accepting the faulty technology of nuclear power generation which it received from the United States; and it built as many as 54 nuclear reactors based on the nuclear fuel cycle. Although Japan has had its three non-nuclear principles (not to make or possess nuclear weapons, and not to allow their entry into Japan) and although it was the only country ever to be attacked with the atomic bombs, it accepted the technology of nuclear power generation, under the impressive phrase "peaceful use of nuclear energy." I wonder if Japan can change itself in the way of Germany, which has decided to close its nuclear plants. A group of politicians, bureaucrats, experts from the electric power companies' special interest group long ignored the opinions from the outside that had pointed out the dangers of producing nuclear energy. This led to the catastrophic accidents. How shall we get the true information about the various problems that have been disclosed so that we may adequately deal with the situation? The questions raised by these 218 poets are concerned with humankind as a whole, thus transcending their individual positions. They attempt to discuss fundamental topics, ranging from those about life in the universe to the present and future of Earth.

The Hanford nuclear site is a mere 200 miles from Portland where Ms. Stenson resides. I understand that there is a high incidence of radiation-induced cancers in the site's vicinity. Ms. Stenson no doubt regards the pain of the people of Hiroshima and Nagasaki, and of Fukushima, as something close at hand, rather than as simply an issue pertaining to others. So that she could see conditions at Fukushima first-hand, I introduced her to Jotaro Wakamatsu of Minamisoma and to Masayuki Nemoto, who was evacuated to Soma from Namiemachi. It was Mr. Nemoto who obtained permission for us to visit Namiemachi, which is just as empty today as it was immediately after the accident. We visited the shopping district near Namiemachi Station. We also saw the Ukedo district, where 500 people are thought to have perished, and were able to go inside the Ukedo Elementary School, which is situated on the coast at a distance of only four kilometers from the Fukushima power plant. In addition to Leah and her husband William, we were joined by their daughter Marisa, who acted as our interpreter. These three people were among the very few, if any, Americans to set foot inside this zone seriously devastated by radiation. I was delighted that they had the opportunity to speak at length with these two poets of Fukushima.

I think that the Americans who contributed to the Japanese edition—Gary Snyder, David Krieger, and Teresinka Pereirad—as well as Ms. Stenson, who conceived of the American edition—are able to transcend national boundaries through poetry. Mr. Krieger, in concert with the volume *Against Nuclear Weapons: A Collection of Poems by 181 Poets,* published *God's Tears: Reflections on the Atomic Bombs Dropped on Hiroshima and Nagasaki,* which was put out by Coal Sack. In addition, he provided commentary for the Japanese anthology *Farewell to Nuclear...*and the American anthology *Reverberations from Fukushima*. I am convinced that borders can only be transcended by means of profound spiritual exchange between individuals.

I hope that this volume will be read not just by those who love poetry, but by people in the United States who, like Roethke, possess an impartial spirit of love for nature and modern civilization.

NOTE: The original Japanese version of Hisao Suzuki's preface was published in *Coal Sack* (No. 77). Due to limitations of space, an edited and abridged version of the Japanese preface is presented in this anthology.

THE POWER OF IMAGINATION

Asao Sarukawa Aroldi

On March 11, 2011, Japan was struck by an earthquake and tsunami the likes of which no Japanese alive today has ever experienced. This disaster was followed almost immediately by the Fukushima nuclear disaster. For a time, the eyes of every Japanese and people around the world were riveted on the Tohoku region, and on Fukushima. Faced with daily television and newspapers reports on the sweeping extent of the damage, and confronted with gruesome catastrophic images of destruction, we were at loss for words. People contributed money to charities and participated in volunteer activities in the hope of somehow helping even a little. "Save Electricity" was the key phrase repeated in every household and workplace, as everyone sacrificed for the common good, and people gathered for antinuclear demonstrations on the streets of Tokyo and in many major cities across Japan. During the months that followed the disaster, there was an almost palpable sense of impeding crisis and grief as our thoughts were extended to the people of Tohoku and Fukushima.

Six months passed, and then a year. Now, as we are poised to mark the third anniversary of March 11, it is time to ask ourselves whether we possess the necessary power of imagination to understand the reality that is unfolding in Fukushima. Moreover, to what extent do people around the world possess the power of imagination to understand that nuclear power is a pressing issue that has direct bearing on their daily lives?

It is said that the ability to forget is a mechanism of the human mind for preserving sanity. Even shocking news-feeds about the alarming conditions at the Fukushima Nuclear Power Plant cease to have impact when we hear them day after day. Amid the daily hustle and bustle, even fear of radiation becomes dulled. This tendency to forget may be said to be the nature of human beings. But we should not forget that while our ability to think and make judgements is thus dulled, the politicians and bureaucrats, the power company, and all those who directly or indirectly profit from the nuclear industry have been busy covering up inconvenient facts, even going so far as to alter existing laws and regulations. We must remember that their first priority is not necessarily protecting people's lives or the environment.

Unleashing the power of imagination is key to reclaiming our integrity, so as not to lower ourselves to the point of becoming people who end up serving the interests of the system, even if we are co-opted into doing so unconsciously. In other words, the power of imagination will help us in our endeavor to understand others, to put ourselves in their place, and to cultivate the power of judgment needed to discern what is important in order that we all might lead a more humane existence.

In Hisao Suzuki's introductory essay in *Farewell to Nuclear, Welcome to Renewable Energy: A Collection of Poems by 218 Poets*, the work on which *Reverberations from Fukushima: 50 Poets Speak Out* is based, poets are characterized as "people who are sensitive to the coming and going of the seasons and the changes in nature," and people who possess the "power to foresee the crises and feel anxiety for the future of humankind and earth."* Such "keen power of observing nature" and "prophetic instinct" are abilities that appear, no doubt, precisely when the power of imagination is present.

Decades prior to the event, poets with highly developed sensitivity composed poems foreseeing the accident at the Fukushima nuclear power plant. In "A Land of Sorrow: A City Spirited Away by God," Jotaro Wakamatsu, who visited Chernobyl in 1994, writes, "People's lives disappeared entirely from a city," describing how the zone within a 30-kilometer radius of the nuclear power plant had been designated as a danger zone resulting in the evacuation of approximately 150,000 residents.

Where should we go and disappear?
Where should we make ourselves disappear?

This question asked by the people of Chernobyl, who had no choice but to wholly abandon the place they were used to living, along with their lives up to that point, was now being repeated word for word in Fukushima.

In "A Letter from the Shroud" (first published in 2002), a poem written about an American nuclear power plant worker who accused the Tokyo Electric Power Company of having concealed the existence of a major crack in the reactor vessel shroud at the Fukushima Nuclear Power Plant, Hisao Suzuki deftly observes:

Without a climate where problems can be made public,
the day will surely come when northeastern Japan is laid waste like Chernobyl.

In his "The Walls" (first published in 2007), Kazunari Usuki, speaks in an eerily prophetic voice:

* *Farewell to Nuclear, Welcome to Renewable Energy: A Collection of Poems by 218 Poets* (ed. Hisao Suzuki et al.), Tokyo: Coal Sack Publishing Company, 2012, p. 289.

However, just as life
one day reaches completion
on account of the death that it contains,
these walls are destined
to break down because of what they contain.
Only then
will we see the real face
of what has been concealed
behind so many walls.

He speaks here of the walls that cloak nuclear reactors. But this could also be taken to mean the walls of the "myth of safety" fabricated by the promoters of nuclear power.

In "If Man Snatches the Fire" (first published in 2008), Eiji Kuroha cites the names of places stricken with disaster as a result of nuclear power plant accidents or nuclear experiments:

Nevada, Bikini, Kazakhstan, Taklamakan Desert,
Three Mile Island, Chernobyl, X, Y and Z.

And we know that X in this series has been replaced with Fukushima. He concludes the poem saying,

...man can't stop himself from pursuing convenience,
because he is aware that the day of his own extinction is approaching.

The common themes that unite the 50 poems by the 50 poets represented in this volume are profound sorrow toward the reality of Fukushima where suffering continues to this day, resentment toward politics that is filled with deceit and toward a society that is indifferent to the plight of the weak and vulnerable, and a requiem for lives lost. Whether we can truly take to heart the words of these poems woven from the experiences and reflections of the poets depends on our sensitivity and our power of imagination. As Kenichi Saso asks in "The Sound of Waves X," "The mind—has it evolved?"

Although I am not endowed with the prophetic instinct of a poet, March 11 has become a turning point for me in many ways. It has become an opportunity for me to reconsider the world in which I live. I now see darker forces at play and can understand that the vested interests of politics and money in Japan and the United States do not necessarily serve the interests of humanity. I now understand the connections between the nuclear power industry, academia and the mainstream media, and cannot help but feel as if I am confronted with what Kazunari Uzuki refers to as the "real face" scowling darkly from between the cracks that have emerged from the distortions of our society.

Needless to say, this state of affairs does not apply only to Japan. Hopefully, Americans, who have the largest nuclear power industry in the world, will come to recognize nuclear power as an imminent personal threat. Steps toward such an understanding could come in the form of calculating the distance from their town to the nearest nuclear power plant or nuclear facility. It could mean putting themselves in the shoes of a mother who cannot sleep at night out of fear and self-reproach over finding a lump in the thyroid of her child; or it could mean reflecting on the agony of a livestock farmer who has to slaughter the animals he raised from birth. If people can cultivate the power of imagination then they can understand that the nuclear problem is their own. If they can't, we will all be headed for a dark future indeed.

Reading poetry is an exercise in extending one's power of imagination. Hopefully, reading the 50 poems in this anthology will enhance your power of imagination. I'm thankful that it enhanced mine.

Essays

TEN LESSONS FROM CHERNOBYL AND FUKUSHIMA

By David Krieger

President of the Nuclear Age Peace Foundation (www.wagingpeace.org), author of numerous books and articles on peace and nuclear weapons abolition, and author of three books of poetry: *Today Is Not a Good Day for War; The Doves Flew High; and God's Tears: Reflections on the Atomic Bombs Dropped on Hiroshima and Nagasaki.*

George Santayana famously said, "Those who cannot remember the past are condemned to repeat it." The same may be said of those who fail to understand the past or to learn from it. If we failed to learn from the nuclear power plant accident at Chernobyl more than a quarter century ago or to understand its meaning for our future, perhaps the more recent accident at Fukushima will serve as a reminder. Here are ten lessons drawn from the Chernobyl and Fukushima disasters.

1. **Nuclear power is a highly complex, expensive and dangerous way to boil water.** Nuclear power does nothing more than provide a high-tech and extremely dangerous way to boil water to create steam to turn turbines.

2. **Accidents happen and the worst-case scenario often turns out to be worse than imagined or planned for.** Although the nuclear industry continues to assure the public that the plants are safe, the plants continue to have accidents, some of which exceed worst-case projections.

3. **The nuclear industry and its experts cannot plan for every contingency or prevent every disaster.** Although it was known that Fukushima is subject to earthquakes and tsunamis, the nuclear industry and its experts did not plan for the combination of a 9.0 earthquake and the larger-than-expected tsunami that followed.

4. **Governments do not effectively regulate the nuclear industry to assure the safety of the public.** Government regulators of nuclear industry often come from the nuclear industry and tend to be too close to the industry to regulate it effectively.

5. **Hubris, complacency and high-level radiation are a deadly mix.** Hubris on the part of the nuclear industry and its government

regulators, along with complacency on the part of the public, have led to the creation of vast amounts of high-level radiation that must be guarded from release to the environment for tens of thousands of years, far longer than civilization has existed.

6. **Nuclear power plants can catastrophically fail, causing vast human and environmental damage. The corporations that run the power plants, however, are protected from catastrophic economic failure by government limits on liability, which shift the economic burden to the public.** If the corporations that own nuclear power plants had to bear the burden of potential financial losses in the event of a catastrophic accident, they would not build the plants because they know the risks are unacceptable. It is government liability limits, such as the Price-Anderson Act in the US, that make nuclear power plants possible, leaving the taxpayers responsible for the overwhelming monetary costs of nuclear industry failures. No other private industry is given such liability protection.

7. **Radiation releases from nuclear accidents cannot be contained in space and will not stop at national borders.** The wind will carry long-lived radioactive materials around the world and affect the people and environment of many countries and regions. The radiation will also affect the oceans of the world, which are the common heritage of humankind.

8. **Radiation releases from nuclear accidents cannot be contained in time and will adversely affect countless future generations.** The radioactive materials from nuclear power plant accidents, as well as from radioactive wastes, are a legacy we are bequeathing to future generations of humans and other forms of life on the planet.

9. **Nuclear energy, as well as nuclear weapons, and human beings cannot co-exist without the risk of future catastrophes.** The survivors of the atomic bombings of Hiroshima and Nagasaki have long known that nuclear weapons and human beings cannot co-exist. The Fukushima accident, like that at Chernobyl before it, makes clear that human beings and nuclear power plants also cannot co-exist without courting future disasters.

10. **The accidents at Fukushima and Chernobyl are a wake-up call to phase out nuclear energy and replace it with**

energy conservation and more human- and environmentally-friendly forms of renewable energy. For decades it has been clear that various forms of renewable energy are needed to replace both nuclear and fossil fuel energy sources. Now it is clearer than ever. The choice is not between nuclear and fossil fuels. The solution is to disavow both of these forms of energy and to move as rapidly as possible to a global energy plan based upon various forms of renewable energy: solar cells, wind, geothermal, ocean thermal, currents, tides, etc.

The nuclear power plant accident at Chernobyl was repeated, albeit with a different set of circumstances, at Fukushima. Have our societies yet learned any lessons from Chernobyl and Fukushima that will prevent the people of the future from experiencing such devastation? As poet Maya Angelou points out, "History, despite its wrenching pain, cannot be unlived, but if faced with courage doesn't need to be lived again." We need the courage to phase out nuclear power globally and replace it with energy conservation and renewable energy sources. In doing so, we will not only be acting responsibly with regard to nuclear power, but will also reduce the risks of nuclear weapons proliferation and strengthen the global foundations for the abolition of these weapons.

THOUGHTS ON THE FIRST NUCLEAR DISASTER OF THE 21ST CENTURY

Francesca Giovannini
Affiliate to the Center for International Security and Cooperation (CISAC) at Stanford University and to Managing the Atom (MTA), Belfer Center for Science and International Affairs, Harvard University.

It is always challenging to write sensibly about an accident that dramatically impacts the life of so many as is the case with the tragedy of Fukushima Dai-ichi.

An array of academic essays and blog articles has materialized in the aftermath of the accident to shed light on the main causes that have led Japan to suffer one of the worst nuclear disasters in history, second only to Chernobyl, Russia in 1985. Although the writings on Fukushima comprehensively examine the political dynamics of the accident, they significantly overlook the depth, severity and gravity of the tragedy experienced by the people of the Fukushima prefecture.

This anthology of poems comes at a critical time and serves as an important reminder that the Fukushima accident must be discussed as more than simply a political and technological failure for it is also a personal tragedy with many victims who are still unable to return to their homes and lands.

These short introductory remarks have been written with two goals in mind. On the one hand, I hope to provide a fair and balanced account of what happened in Fukushima Daiichi during and after the nuclear accident in March 2011. On the other hand, I seek to underscore the significance of the contribution made by this anthology by contextualizing it in the current political debate that is taking place in Japan over the sustainability of nuclear energy.

Although some questions remain unanswered at present, the overall dynamics of the Fukushima accident are clear. When the most powerful earthquake in Japanese history struck at 2.46 pm on March 11, 2011, the three operating units of the Fukushima nuclear plant immediately shut down automatically. The tsunami that struck the plant one hour after the earthquake, however, breached the plant's inadequate seawall and flooded the basement where off-site generator batteries were stored (a violation of basic nuclear safety principles) and disabled the plant's cooling system. This led to a meltdown of the fuel and an explosion of excess hydrogen, which was captured on camera.

In the months that followed the accident, the causes of the Fukushima disaster became an issue for national political dispute and divergent voices emerged to characterize Fukushima either as a man-made disaster or simply as a tragedy brought about by an unpredictable natural cataclysm. The truth probably lies somewhere in the middle. While it is true that the combination of natural factors (an earthquake of unprecedented magnitude followed by a tsunami) was not only difficult to predict but almost impossible to confront, the forces of nature were undoubtedly exacerbated by the complacency that had been building for years among Japanese leaders vis-a-vis the management of nuclear technology. The tolerance in Japan towards the existence of a powerful "nuclear village," a conglomerate of political groups, private sector, media, academic institutions, nuclear vendors and utilities all interested in maintaining and running the nuclear sector, led to a remarkable decline in nuclear safety preparedness and the absence of independent oversight to nuclear governance in the country. In addition, in order to maintain public support for nuclear energy, the nuclear village adopted strategies to perpetuate the so-called "myth of absolute safety." Although emergency plans had been designed in case of a nuclear accident, for example, they were never tested so as to not contradict the idea that nuclear energy was safe and reliable. The failure of this system was inevitable; it was only a matter of when and how.

Immediately following the accident and the consequent release of radioactive material, the government ordered the evacuation of approximately 78,000 people living within 20 kilometers from the plant and recommended the sheltering of an additional 62,000 people within a 30 kilometer radius of the plant. Nearly two years after the accident, it is unclear how many people have returned to their homes despite government warnings. What we do know, however, is that a high level of radiation persists in several areas around the Fukushima prefecture (which used to be the third most populated area in Japan) hence preventing many from coming back. Land has also been contaminated and has imposed severe costs to food producers and farmers who are now demanding compensation from TEPCO, the nuclear operator of the Fukushima plant.

Very little attention is currently devoted in Japan and elsewhere to discussing and understanding the misfortune of the people of Fukushima and their ongoing suffering. The politicization of the debate about the causes of the accident and the future of nuclear energy in Japan has diverted public attention away from the tragedy of tens of thousands losing their homes, their land and their memories.

Why is the narrative around Fukushima almost entirely centered on political and technical considerations? The accident of Fukushima has brought to light the deficiencies and incompetency long tolerated within the Japanese nuclear safety system. In response to and in consideration of its reputation nationally and internationally, the Japanese nuclear industry acted quickly to regain its credibility among stakeholders by accepting responsibility and demonstrating its commitment to accountability and transparency. Therefore, the political process following the accident has focused on identifying political and institutional solutions to better regulate the nuclear sector rather than working to implement the necessary social conditions for people of Fukushima to heal and overcome the trauma of the accident.

In the past two years, the Japanese government has attempted to address some of the concerns raised both domestically and internationally. It has responded by undertaking reforms such as halting, at least temporarily, the 52 operative nuclear reactors in the country and creating new regulatory institutions to oversee the governance of nuclear energy in the country. Nevertheless, the significance of the accident of Fukushima, the first nuclear disaster of the 21st century, has global repercussions.

Firstly, the way in which the world is responding to the nuclear accident in Fukushima seems to suggest that, in general, the world has become more tolerant towards the risks embedded in the use of powerful technologies such as the nuclear power generation. Unlike the accident at the Chernobyl plant, which virtually halted the construction of many nuclear reactors around the world, the devastation that resulted from the Fukushima accident has only had a minimal impact on the prospect for new nuclear builds around the world. The International Atomic Energy Agency (IAEA), which serves as the global nuclear watchdog, has estimated that only 2% of the pre-Fukushima planned nuclear construction has been suspended. This trend begs a pressing question: has the world become more risk-tolerant vis-a-vis technologies such as nuclear that would have been questioned in years past? And, if so, what has brought about this more accommodating attitude? Is it social changes in the way in which societies perceive risks and benefits, or simply economic and energy considerations that drive such a complacent attitude?

Secondly, as the Fukushima accident has shown, the safeguards established during the construction of nuclear facilities several years ago are no longer sufficient to protect against potential natural disasters. The magnitude and scale of many natural hazards today require a serious reevaluation of the physical protection of many nuclear facilities around the world. Above all it requires a global political conversation on whether such a powerful and perilous technology such as nuclear can be managed safely in the natural environment that keeps changing. Yet incentives for such a global conversation to occur are largely nonexistent today as countries struggle to ensure energy security and compete for increasingly scarce resources.

While this all pertains to high politics, and to broader conversations about what we eternally refer to as the global nuclear order, returning to the human dimension of the Fukushima accident is necessary, important and above all just. It reminds us that in a world that prides itself on skillful development and technological innovation, one mistake may bear catastrophic consequences for all of humanity. It is also important to remember that while we explore and develop new technologies, our innovations have to be integrated and accommodated in an increasingly unstable natural environment. This requires global cooperation based on a common sense of humanity and our shared vision for a more sustainable world.

Fifty Poems by 50 Poets

Hisao Suzuki (1954-) Born in Tokyo. Lives in Kashiwa, Chiba.

A LETTER FROM THE SHROUD

Even now big waves may be surging upon the shores
of Fukushima where my father and mother were born.
Waves dragged me as a boy to the sandy bottom of the sea,
making me gulp down brine, and then cast me ashore.

Are waves still cooling the heated water discharged from the nuclear
power plant?
What prompts men to become inured to madness?
When the man falsified the inspection data,
he must have felt a sting of conscience in his heart.
His heart may have almost burst because of the lie,
and he may have lost sleep on account of heat and fatigue in the
reactor's shroud.

In July 2000,
the man was afraid the crack in the shroud might get larger and burst open.
Someone on the inside charged that Tokyo Electric Power Company
had been hiding the crack for ten years,
and two year later, in August 2002, the charge was found to be true.

I would like to inquire about the conflicts in the man's heart.
I would like to praise the heroic and conscientious act of the informer.
Without a climate where problems can be made public,
the day will surely come when northeastern Japan is laid waste like
Chernobyl.
Six reactors in the Fukushima No. 1 nuclear power plant.
Four reactors in the Fukushima No. 2 nuclear power plant.
Three reactors in the Niigata Kashiwazaki Kariwa nuclear power plant.
Of the 13 reactors, five are being operated with cracks, unrepaired,
by the Nuclear and Industrial Safety Agency and Tokyo Electric Power
Company.
The status of the remaining eight reactors is also dubious.

The government and electric power companies never tell the truth.
Organizations continue hiding the faults in their technology.
When will the next letter come from the reactor's shroud
to the people along the shores of Fukushima and Niigata?
Will the next letter that comes tell how cracks in the reactor's shroud

have grown into cracks in the entire structure of deteriorating nuclear
    technology?

When I played on the beach in Fukushima as a boy, there were no
    nuclear power plants.
How many thousands of years will it take for the beach of my
    childhood to be restored?
Will that man's name be inscribed on an anti-nuclear monument on
    that beach in the future?
And will children be playing in the waves around it?

(First appeared in 2002)

Translated by Naoshi Koriyama

Kazunari Usuki (1961-) Born in Kagoshima. Lives in Ibusuki, Kagoshima.

THE WALLS

It was unusually chilly
and it was raining in June.
A man hanged himself in a small apartment.
Just as he had promised his sweetheart,
he died leaving a fantastic suicide note: *I'll die for you.*

You mutter that tragedy is beautiful
because you are carrying death within life

and because you are intensely conscious of death
while living.

As the skull envelopes the brain,
a person envelopes death
in a wall known as the body.
Even so, life is tinged
with the faint smell of death
leaking from within.

The ground around Hokusatsu holds pellet-sized ore of uranium.
It is said that the foundation of a nuclear power plant is anchored
directly to the bedrock to make it earthquake-proof.
And it is surrounded by multiple layers of walls
that hold the radioactive materials.

However, just as life
one day reaches completion
on account of the death it contains,
these walls are destined
to break down because of what they contain.
Only then
will we see the real face
of what has been concealed
behind so many walls.

(First published in the October, 2007 issue of Shi to Shiso.)

Translated by Naoshi Koriyama

Eiji Kuroha (1931-) Born in Tokyo. Lives in Naka, Kanagawa.

IF A MAN SNATCHES FIRE

It was the people of Qi who worried,
fearing that Heaven might tumble down.
And now I live in a depressing valley in Shimizu, Higashi-Koiso, Ohiso,
deploring that we are trapped in the Age of the Atom
and can no longer return to the Primitive Age.

I think of the sun, a stupendous ball of fire with a radius of 700,000 km,
floating in empty space,
continuously emitting temperatures of 15 million degrees
and producing a super high-pressure of 100 billion atmospheres.

Man stole the secret from the hands of the god of fire,
and used low-level enriched uranium for nuclear reactors,
and highly enriched uranium for nuclear weapons,
and produced enormous amount of energy through the chain reaction
of atomic fission.

But, he dropped "Little Boy" on Hiroshima,
and "Fat Man" on Nagasaki,
not only destroying hundreds of thousands of human lives instantly,
but also continuing to kill 200,000 people in Hiroshima
and 140,000 in Nagasaki
in the five years that followed.

To prevent uranium or plutonium from reacting with the coolants,
he processed the fuel by covering it with a thin film of metal,
and to contain radioactivity,
he used a nuclear reactor to produce nuclear fission and make fuel.

To recover uranium and plutonium from the spent nuclear fuel,
he built a spent fuel reprocessing plant in Tokai Mura,
which began trial operations in 1977.
And just when the Tokai plant reached full operational capacity,
a catastrophic disaster occurred in Chernobyl; an infinite dread.
This revealed the despairing reality
that we are trapped in the Age of the Atom and can no longer return
to the Primitive Age.

Nevada, Bikini, Kazakhstan, Taklamakan Desert,

Three Mile Island, Chernobyl, X, Y and Z.
Diving under the sea, flying in the sky, soaring out into space,
man can't stop himself from pursuing convenience,
because he is aware that the day of his own extinction is approaching.

(First appeared around 2008)

Translated by Naoshi Koriyama

Fumiko Suzuki (1942-) Born in Chiba. Lives in Abiko, Chiba.

ON THE NIGHT MARKING SUMMER'S END

—A nuclear nomad passes away—

He was a good guy, wasn't he?
Yeah, he sure was.
And he liked to drink, didn't he?
He had nothing to do but drink, you know.

How many years ago did he quit farming?
It's been five years since his farm filled up with weeds.
It's been three and a half years since he quit fishing.
No catch in the sea for a long time, burdened with debts,
there was nothing he could do.
Then,
a contractor boss came along.
Working for ten or twenty minutes, or sometimes only three minutes,
he could earn a day's wages.
For a man who had risked his life fishing
the job at the nuclear power plant seemed like a God-send.

It was the same with the farmers.
Not knowing anything,
they donned rubber raincoats, high boots,
and masks like spacemen.
Since the masks were uncomfortable, they took them off and kept working.
On one occasion,
as I mopped up water on the floor of the nuclear plant,
the dosimeter alarm hanging on my chest
made such an irritating noise, going "peee... peee..."
We worked on, without paying attention to such things.

That's right.
Even if the needle went clear off the scale
we couldn't quit the job.
We needed the money.
The only thing I worried about was losing my job the next day.
When the day's work was done
I simply wrote *120 millirems* in the report
—the permissible radiation level.

It is said that if the radiation level goes over 200 millirems
the meter's needle will swing past the maximum.
We can't see radiation,
nor can we smell it.
When we were working,
no part of our bodies hurt,
so it's hard to believe it's dangerous.
Do you remember that black guy?
He was big and had white teeth
and he'd say, *konichiwa.*
Konichiwa and *sayonara* were the only Japanese words he knew.
Moving his body rhythmically, he talked a lot.
He was a friendly good-natured young man.
Spreading his arms open wide,
bending his neck a bit,
he'd say, *sayonara.*
I hear that he was exposed to 1,000 millirems of radiation
in the cracked reactor.
I wonder if he got home safely.
Since he was young and his skin was shining,
I guess he didn't feel any bad effects.
Surely, he didn't feel it.

He was a good guy, wasn't he?
Yeah,
pretty soon we too will be gone.
Well, shall we have a drink?
Yeah.....

Note: "Rem" is a unit for measuring the level of radiation. (Now "sievert" is used). The upper limit of annual radiation exposure for nuclear plant workers is 500 millirems, as stipulated by Japanese law. This is an unacceptably high level of radiation exposure.

(This poem was published in the first issue of *Kaifu*, 1987.)

Translated by Naoshi Koriyama

Mariko Fukuda (1933-2006) Born in Tokyo. Lived in Hirakata, Osaka.

SITE WHERE DANGEROUS OBJECTS ARE BURIED

You can't pick raspberries
or make raspberry preserves from an area
tainted with radioactivity from nuclear power.
You have to kill all those birds and animals
now dancing before your eyes
and bury them in a dark hole.
"Site Where Dangerous Objects Are Buried"—What a chilling sign!
Such dreadful things are unheard of even in the old tales of hell.
Full of life, the flowery fields of spring
all at once shed blood and died—
not only died but also continued burning with vengeful thoughts.
"Site Where Dangerous Objects Are Buried"—
You can neither go into the woods
nor cleanse your heart by picnicking in the fields.
You fear the direction of the wind from where the cesium flowers bloom.
Those who have gone there, never return.
How would you explain to God
what mankind has done
to repeat such a stupid act
causing those who go there to never return?
The question is in the eyes of a young girl.
Indeed, how would you explain it?
Isn't it said that
emotion makes life meaningful
when we recollect the old days?
Five-year-olds listen to the news. Six-year-olds walk in demonstrations.
Seven-year-olds worry about the contamination of sand, cars, and flowers.
...so reported the West German weekly magazine *Stern.*
Hearts of little children ought to be filled
with little pleasures,
but now there are no pleasures like secret gardens in the woods or parks.
"Site Where Dangerous Objects Are Buried"—
The harsh sight of this sign brings foreboding that ripples darkly.
From which direction does the wind blow today?
There are no more stories for children here.

Translated by Aya Yuhki

Yukari Mutou (1965-) Born in Ibaraki. Lives in Naka, Ibaraki.

FRESH AIR

Hey there, elderly gentleman,
would you please close the windows.
There was an accident at the nearby plant
and radioactive material is in the air.

> *Ha ha ha.*
> *Dear Nurse,*
> *It's hot today, I tell you.*
> *We need fresh air! Fresh air!*

Mister,
It's dangerous to keep the windows open.
The official report warned about it, you know.

> *Ha ha ha.*
> *But I can't stand the smell,*
> *because that guy wet his pants, you know.*

But, it's not good to breathe in the outside air.
How can I make you understand it?

> *Dear Nurse,*
> *nothing is in the air, you see.*
> *Ha ha ha.*

Reprinted from a book of verse, *Sand and Stars* (January, 2000)

Translated by Naoshi Koriyama

Rumiko Kora (1932-) Born in Tokyo. Lives in Meguro, Tokyo.

TO GIVE BIRTH

I'm not sure whether I heard it, or not,
that the Chinese character 産む "to give birth" depicts a woman giving birth in a sitting position.*
At a childbearing hut remaining
in a village where a nuclear power plant has been built
an old woman talks
about the childbearing that used to occur there.
A rope for a woman to pull on, to strain her body in childbearing,
hangs from the ceiling.
Twenty-four small bundles of straw
are piled up against each other on the sand.
The woman leans on the bundles of straw,
grabs the rope, raising her body.
Dark gray waves of the Japan Sea break on the shore.
Falling snow disappears in the sea.
A road resembling a birth canal crosses the village.
Women have given birth to children in this way
and have kept on bearing children,
but the road always leads people in unexpected directions.
People have come to a dead end—
separated from one another, lost,
caught up in a dark whirlpool,
losing sight of their way home,
they stand alone in a daze.

I'm not sure whether I heard it, or not,
that the element 生 in the character 産 (to give birth)
depicts a baby being born.
In the childbearing hut where light enters only from the sea,
the woman, who has given birth to four children, says
If you press on the anus with your heel,
you can prevent the baby from going back to the womb.
A narrow stream flows in front of the hut.
She washes rice and cooks it there.

In the olden days, when a woman left the hut after childbirth,
she ducked under the waves and swam through the waves

* The traditional way of childbearing was in a sitting position.

at dawn on the shore of the Japan Sea
to return from death.*

Women have given birth in this way,
have kept on giving birth, but the birth canal has eventually led
to the nuclear power plant, has it not?
Because we did not make an effort to determine where the road was
leading us,
those giving birth and those being born have become separated.
Each of us now travels the road alone in the gathering dusk,
but the image of a woman giving birth
remains transfixed within the form of the Chinese character.

(This poem first appeared in the November-December 1983 issue of *Shin Nihon Bungaku*.)

Translated by Naoshi Koriyama

---

* The woman needed to be cleansed by the waves of the ocean because giving birth also meant going to the afterworld in order to give birth to a new life—in the cycle of life and death.

Jotaro Wakamatsu (1935-) Born in Iwate. Lives in Minami-Soma, Fukushima.

A LAND OF SORROW: A CITY SPIRITED AWAY BY GOD

A Litany (6)

45,000 human beings disappeared in two hours.
This wasn't from a sports arena after the conclusion of a soccer match.
People's lives disappeared entirely from a city.
The radio sounded the warning to evacuate:
Take enough food for three days!
Many people hoped that they could return home in three days.
Some carrying small bags, an old lady holding a kitten,
patients undergoing treatment at hospitals, all riding aboard 1,100 buses.
45,000 human beings disappeared in two hours.
Happy voices of children playing tag,
greetings between neighbors over fences,
the ringing bell on the mailman's bicycle,
the smell of borsch cooking,
lights out of windows at night,
people's daily lives,
the entire city of Pripyat disappeared from the map.
That is what happened within 40 hours after the Chernobyl nuclear
accident.
Riding on 1,100 buses,
the citizens of Pripyat City dispersed in two hours,
and together with three neighboring villages,
altogether 49,000 people disappeared.
49,000 is about the same
as the population of Haramachi City where I live.
And then,
the zone within a 30-km radius of the nuclear power plant
was designated as a danger zone,
and within three days after May 6, the 11th day after the notice,
92,000 people evacuated,
bringing the total number of evacuees to some 150,000
People dispersed, disappearing into farming villages 100 or 150 km away.
The zone within a 30-km radius
of the Tokyo Electric Power Company's Fukushima nuclear power plant
includes the towns of Futaba, Okuma, Tomioka, Naraha, Namie and Hirono,
and the villages of Kawauchi, Miyakoji, Katsurao and
Odaka, the northern part of Iwaki City,

and the city of Haramachi where I live.
Altogether the population of these districts is also about one hundred-fifty thousand.
Where should we go and disappear?
Where should we make ourselves disappear?
Even 6 years after the Chernobyl accident some people were ordered to evacuate their villages.
Eight years after the accident
we enter the former city of Pripyat.
Weeds grow wildly
through the cracks, elbowing the cracks aside.
Swallows fly. Pidgeons sit with bulging chests.
Butterflies rest their wings on the flowers.
Flies move around uneasily.
Swarms of mosquitoes swirl.
Leaves of boulevard trees yield themselves to the wind.
Yet,
it is a city with no human voices.
It is a city where no human walks.
It is a city where 45,000 people are hiding.
I look all around in earnest pursuit.
Toys scattered around in the kindergarten's hall,
a stewpot left on the stove in the kitchen,
papers spread open on the desks in the office—
there are signs that people were here just a few moments ago.
But the sun is setting.
I, despite my earnest pursuit, am at a loss.
All the friends have been spirited away by some god
and I stand transfixed on a plaza all alone.
Department stores, hotels,
cultural centers, schools, apartment houses—all are breaking down.
Everything is headed for ruin,
competing with human lives
and the city built by humans in the race to ruin are:
strontium 90 with its half-life of 27.7 years
cesium 137 with its half-life of 30 years
plutonium 239 with its half-life of 24,400 years.
It takes 90 years for the radiation level of cesium to go down to 1/8.
Cesium with a radiation level 8 times above the lethal level will continue killing living things for the next 90 years from now.
If men cannot handle things that will occur one hundred years in the future,
it is arrogant for them to handle plutonium now, is it not?
I walk on the grounds of the abandoned kindergarten.

I step into the weeds.
Nuclides sticking to the weeds must have been blown around.
Lungs must have inhaled the air in which the nuclides are mixed.
More cities may be spirited away by ghosts on Earth.
We may be spirited away even today.
Sensing children's voices behind me,
I turn around, but there is no one.
I feel a shiver go down my spine.
I continue standing alone on the plaza.

(First published in 1994.)

Translated by Naoshi Koriyama

Makoto Yoshida (1933-1987) Born and died in Fukushima.

HEAVY DAYS AND YEARS

The shoreline of my hometown has become the Ginza* of nuclear
    power,
and the simple life of the people
and even the look in their eyes has somehow changed
in these ten years.

As the length of our lives is limited,
these ten years have been long for everyone.
But
if we hadn't run around raising money, which we weren't accustomed to,
if we hadn't collected signatures, or attended study meetings
for these past ten years,
our lives would have been empty and poor.

Even so, the decision of the court was arrogant.
Where did our sense of futility come from?
Was it because the judges turned their heads away from the truth?
Or was it because they flattered authority?

It's they that were arrogant,
not us.

The "truth" has always been in the minority,
just as we are now.

Someday nuclear power
will certainly turn its fangs on people.
We should keep a steady eye
on this savage beast.
To forever reject this monster—
therein lies our raison d'etre.

If we should be negligent in this
then surely our grandchildren will someday ask:
"What did your generation do?"

(Written: July 23, 1984, when the Fukushima District Court handed down its decision.)

Translated by Naoshi Koriyama

---

* The Ginza is Tokyo's most famous up-market shopping, dining and entertainment district.

Ryu Nishina (1940-) Born in Niigata. Lives in Itabashi, Tokyo.

A PHANTOM COUNTRY OF CIVILIZATION

From Hiroshima to Fukushima

Swallowed up in a muddy stream,
though aware of the foolishness of the country's policies,
the people of this country chose, without logic, the way of darkness.
They knew no way other than fighting with bamboo spears
against heavily-equipped invading forces,
thus incurring the dropping of atomic bombs,
and being knocked out, until they came to their senses in the
burned-out land.
Didn't this country come trudging along,
carrying the darkness of Hiroshima and Nagasaki on its back?

A myth about the safety of nuclear power plants had been concocted
and nuclear power plants now jostle each other for space on this island
country.
A colored woodblock print of prosperity was envisioned in swirling greed.
Didn't the people of this country look away
from the real image of history
and just keep walking arrogantly along a new trail of fantasy,
imagining that they had reached the top of the world?
In their arrogance and childishness, they were elated by virtual images,
and now radioactivity is starting to spread
from within their own country.

Hasn't a fatal crumbling begun?
However, just as they once parroted the announcements
from the wartime Imperial Headquarters,
no one is telling the truth about what is happening:
the meltdowns at Fukushima's nuclear power plant.
Powerful hot winds rage through the rift in the airspace.
We stand, powerless and bare-skinned,
in the scorching sunlight.
While radioactivity dances wildly in the wind and light,
no one can see it, or has any way to deal with it.
We stand, motionless, in the flow of time that passes from life to death.

Translated by Naoshi Koriyama

Hiromi Mishou (1925-) Born in Yamaguchi. Lives in Hiroshima.

WHAT SHOULD WE DO?

In the azure sky
shines a bright blue mosque.
I wonder if the stolen Magic Lamp of Aladdin
is still shining now
in the marketplace of Baghdad
that I heard about in my dreams
—in my boyhood—
in the exotic story
of Ali Baba and the Forty Thieves.

Dr. Charmockly of the Pediatrics Department of Baghdad University
Medical College says:
Children suffering from leukemia are overflowing the hospital's hallways.*
What can a doctor without medicines do for them?
What did the doctors in Hiroshima do
for their patients fifty-eight years ago?
Asked these unanswerable questions,
my memory is forever scorched by the flash of that day,
and I just look down speechless.

Children suffering from leukemia, held by young mothers,
smile innocently.
Staring at the photos on my desk of deformed children —
children without brains whose eyes and eyelids protrude,
children with hydrocephalus—
I become blind.

Dr. Al Ali who has come from Basra says:
What can a doctor do
who has no medicines to prescribe?
What did you do?
What do you think can be done?
*I would like to hear your advice, you, the doctor from Hiroshima.***

---

* These children were exposed to radiation from depleted uranium shells fired by US and coalition forces.

** Hiromi Misho, the author of this poem, is himself a *hibakusha* (survivor of the atomic bombings) and a doctor who has dedicated his life to treating A-bomb victims in Hiroshima.

Children are sprawled all over the examination tables.
Is it you, mother, who is whispering
into your child's ear?
Skinny cheeks,
pearl-like eyes.
I gently touch
the tender skin.
It's cold!
The skin is ice-cold.

Translated by Naoshi Koriyama

Hiroyoshi Komatsu (1934-) Born in Kochi. Lives in Kochi.

EINSTEIN'S VOICE

Bamboo poles for sale!
Bamboo poles for sale!"

While I am reading the newspaper, reclining
in the afternoon on a summer's day,
I hear the sing-song cry of a man selling laundry poles.*

The atomic bomb, Little Boy, was dropped on Hiroshima
at 15 minutes and 17 seconds past 9:00 a.m.
August 6, Tinian Time.
It is said
when the news reached Einstein,
who had contributed to the Manhattan Project,
he just uttered a groan:

*Oh weh!***

And
in similar words in a will
he wrote five months before his death:
If I had my life to live over again,
I would like to be a tinsmith or traveling salesman,
not a scientist or a teacher.

Bamboo poles for sale!
Bamboo poles for sale!
Bamboo poles for sale!

No one seems to be buying any bamboo poles.
Outside the windows
the sky is clear, like in Hiroshima.

Oh weh!

Did he turn at the street corner?
The voice of the traveling salesman, Einstein,
is fading further away.

Translated by Naoshi Koriyama

---

* Laundry poles are long bamboo poles (or aluminum poles) used for hanging laundry to dry.

** *Oh Weh* (alternate, Yiddish: Oy vey) is a German / Austrian expression of pain or sadness.

Shizuka Kawana (1936-) Born in Chiba. Lives in Minami-Boso, Chiba.

LIKE TOMATOES

I place the frying pan on the fire, grease it,
and put in some cherry tomatoes.
Their thin skin peals off crisply.

Red flesh is exposed.
Oil soaks in steadily.
Sauce seeps in gradually.
They look hurt.

The skin of *hibakusha* peels off,
dangling from their red flesh.
Their lymph oozes out; they feel thirsty.

On that day, human beings were burned like tomatoes.
The burned tomatoes ran around in disarray
on white feet

as a result of the devil's toy.

Translated by Naoshi Koriyama

Masumi Tanizaki (1934-) Born in Hokkaido. Lives in Sapporo, Hokkaido.

TRANSITION OF A MYTH

Both those who know about Chernobyl
and those who don't know about Chernobyl
are surely now aware of the keen sensitivity
of the tender organs and bones inside of
babies and infants, boys and girls,
which are as mysterious and delicate as eggs.

They built more than a dozen nuclear reactors
along the seacoast without thinking carefully about
what meaning it would really have, and they weren't afraid.

No one has died.
There's nothing particularly wrong.

We already knew of
the wretched spectacle of nuclear testing in the Pacific,
the madness at Semipalatinsk,
and the Iraqi children hit by depleted uranium rounds.

For example, the misery of thyroid cancer
is expressed
by scars on the necks of the children of Chernobyl.

Both those who lived there as well as those who have never lived there
must make sure:
Is the place safe enough for us to return?

Will it turn out to be a myth
that they can return to the place where they were born?

We must keep looking at even what is hidden in the rubble.
We have to discern the words from the silence
of the ripe fruit hanging on the branches.

Translated by Naoshi Koriyama

Masanori Shida (1953-) Born in Nagasaki. Lives in Sasebo, Nagasaki.

HELEN KELLER'S FINGERTIPS

People around me let me touch their faces
without saying anything.

Helen Keller, on a return trip to Japan in 1948,
visited Hiroshima.
She directly touched the A-bomb survivors' keloid scars
and came to understand the horrors of the Atomic Bomb.

For Helen, who had lost her eyesight and hearing,
touch was her only means of knowing the world.
And her thin fingertips could extensively read
the absurdity of humanity
more clearly than the eyes and ears of those who can see and hear.

If Helen were to visit Fukushima now
and touch the ground with her fingertips,
what kind of scream would pierce her skin
and shake her soul?

We cannot see, though we have eyes.
We cannot hear, though we have ears.
Helen's fingertips would point out
the absurdity of trying to rationalize our crime
simply out of attachment to fleeting prosperity.

Ah, I myself would like to touch the ground lovingly
with my own living fingertips
and open my eyes wide and listen attentively with my ears,
and pass the baton to the future with my own hands.

Translated by Naoshi Koriyama

Yasunori Akiyama (1938-) Born in Tokyo. Lives in Matsumoto, Nagano.

GIVE US BACK EVERYTHING

In an abandoned hamlet
several dozens cows
tied to cowsheds died, sprawled on the floor,
leaving tooth-marks on the wooden door frames.

From their parched hide,
from their hooves kicking the air
from the rusty iron beams of the cowshed,
from the dirt of the floor,
from the dent in the roof,
from the roots of the grass, trunks of trees, and the air,
something is silently watching.

The impact of death eating into humanity
has taken its first steps toward eternity.
It pushed up the concrete floors
covering the ground in Hiroshima and Nagasaki,
stood up from the seabed of Bikini Atoll,
let the *Lucky Dragon* drift about,
crushed some humans to death.

We must not be patient.
To be patient is to run away.
To endure is to look away from reality.
When it hurts, we should cry out loudly, *Ouch!*
Crying, *Ouch! Ouch!*
we should locate the source of the pain.

We must not treat those driven from their homes by radioactivity
as an unimportant minority.
We must not keep them waiting.
We should say in unison
to those who hid what they didn't want us to see
and to those who, from the beginning,
treated what shouldn't exist as though it had never existed,
Give us back our cows! Give us back the fodder!
Give us back our homes, farms, grass and trees!
Give us back our water, air, insects, fish and birds!
Give us back our neighbors!

Give us back peace for the babies not yet born!
Give us back everything that once was!
Give us back the future that is yet to come!

Translated by Naoshi Koriyama

Teruyuki Honda (1953-2014) Born in Saitama. Lived in Ichikawa, Chiba.

FUKUSHIMA

At 2:46 p.m., on March 11, 2011,
The earthquake occurred offshore in the Pacific Ocean to the northeast.
Its magnitude was 9.0.

The nuclear reactors at Tokyo Electric Power Fukushima Daiichi
Nuclear Power Station suspended operations immediately.

At 3:27 p.m.,
The first wave of the tsunami struck,
with an estimated height of 15 meters.

Fukushima Reactor 1—
At 3:37 p.m., March 11,
The supply of all alternating current failed.
The ECCS (emergency core cooling system) stopped.
At 5:00 p.m., the same day,
The fuel rods were exposed.
At 8:00 p.m., the same day,
A meltdown occurred.
At 3:36 p.m., March 12, a hydrogen explosion occurred.
At 7:04 p.m., the infusion of sea water began.

Fukushima Reactor 2—
At 3:41 p.m., March 11,
All power failed.
At 1:25 p.m., March 13, the ECCS failed.
At 4:34 p.m., the infusion of sea water began.
At 6:00 p.m., the fuel rods were exposed.
At 11:00 p.m., a meltdown occurred.
At 6:10 a.m., March 15, a hydrogen explosion occurred.
The pressure control room was damaged.

Fukushima Reactor 3—
At 3:38 p.m., March 11,
All power failed.
At 11:36 a.m., March 12,
The ECCS stopped.
At 8:00 a.m., March 13,
The fuel rods were exposed.

At 11:00 a.m., March 14,
A hydrogen explosion occurred.
At 10:00 p.m., a meltdown occurred.

The quantity of radioactivity released into the air
was 770,000 trillion becquerels;
the quantity released into the sea was 4,720 trillion, 1,500 million
becquerels.
On the INES scale,
this was a Level 7 disaster (the highest).
More than120,000 people
fled the exclusion zone.
According to the IAEA,
there has only been a myth of safety,
there has never been a culture of safety.

120,000 tons of highly contaminated water
with 720,000 trillion becquerels remain,
and the contaminated water is increasing by 500 tons every day.
Not only the reactor buildings, but the nuclear reactors themselves
with holes in the hearts of their containment vessels
cannot be buried in the water.
How long should we wait
for their stone coffins to be made?
When can we go to heaven? When?

(Written on June 30, 2011)

Translated by Yorifumi Yaguchi

Hatsuko Hara (1941-) Born in Yamanashi. Lives in Kawagoe, Saitama.

THE DAY MY PROFESSIONAL CAREER ENDED

On August 31, 2011,
my professional career ended.
I retired from my company.

Since March 11, suddenly
my desk was flooded with papers.
I worked till 10:00 or 11:00 p.m. every day.
I went to the company on Saturdays and Sundays.
But on Mondays when I went there, my desk was again full of papers.
I struggled with them every day.
All of these were related to the delivery of electricity.
I no longer saw my husband.
Our two children were left in the care of my mother-in-law.
Believing this was the time to show my true mettle,
I worked and worked till my body couldn't move.

July.
My body gave a warning sign.
When I arrived at the company in the morning, I felt my heart throbbing.
I felt dizzy before the mountains of papers.
I could not write because of the shaking of my hands.
I could not read because the letters seemed covered in mist.
When lunchtime approached, I felt nauseous.
I got off the train at the wrong station.
I thought it was some kind of mistake.
I thought I was losing my mind.
I thought of the day laborers at the nuclear plants.
I thought I had to work harder.
I thought I had to continue working until I finished everything.

I did not tell anyone about it.
I could not tell anyone.
When I entered the company I told my parents,
Father and Mother,
Don't participate in the anti-nuclear movement.
I am a member of Tokyo Electric Power Company.

I could not tell anyone
what my mother said at that time:

It's your life.
Your parents have their own lives.
What is good is good, whoever does it.
What is bad is bad, whoever does it.
The things that people do are not perfect.
A nuclear plant is the same as an atomic bomb.

That time was a glacial period for job hunters.
When I wrote a letter to my teacher, he answered quickly, saying,
Come and see me.
I was so happy.
I was happy because I managed to get a job through my own efforts.
My teacher taught me the relationship between the economy and the environment.
I trusted him.
The location of the interview was the Tokyo Electric Power Company.

My work was fun.
I felt proud to be working for a company that produces electricity.
I found my partner
and bore two children.
All the women who entered the company with me have retired.
The only ones who remain are former high-ranking officials.

My assignment?
I was in charge of the personnel management at the Fukushima Nuclear Power Plant.
But the temporary workers were outside my scope of responsibility.
When the radiation leaked, it was their job.
They were the ones who did the dangerous work.
They cannot work more than two days a week,
since they are constantly exposed to radiation.
Their work history is erased when they retire
because the company would get in trouble
if these records could be used to establish the cause of illness.
Their life
is not the life of the Tokyo Electric Power Company.

Now, I am
a citizen concerned with conserving electricity
so that we can live without nuclear power.

Translated by Yorifumi Yaguchi

Itsuko Ishikawa (1933-) Born in Tokyo. Lives in Katsushika, Tokyo.

CHURCH ROCK & FUKUSHIMA

1.

Is that the faint cry
of a goat, a cow, or a horse
of Church Rock,*
buried alive?

The goat of our neighbor Fanny
was buried thus in the ground
with its forelegs just showing a bit above the mud,
tangled in sticky bentonite.

White men
suddenly came and uprooted the trees,
made holes here and there with dynamite,
and when they finished their work,
they poured bentonite into them.
When Aunt Fanny protested, they answered,
Our president lives beyond where the sun rises.
Please complain to him.

The men dug uranium.
Uranium slag is radioactive for tens of thousands of years
and makes the Navajo suffer from lung cancer.

Aunt Fanny's nine-year-old grandson,
who was playing on the slag heap,
stopped breathing and died one night.

Late at night, Church Rock
is filled with fierce cries of the animals of the earth.
They are like a shower.

Isn't the cry of her grandson mixed in with them?
White-haired Aunt Fanny sits up
on her dark bed. She listens.

---

* Church Rock, New Mexico was the site of extensive uranium mining and is now a Superfund Site.

2.

There is a black plastic bag
that you never leave, not even for a moment.
(Inside it, your hometown is crying.
Your home is angry.)

Someone shouted, *The tsunami is coming!*
Then, in desperate flight, you escaped to higher and higher ground.
You intended to return home after the tsunami,
but then there was the meltdown at the Fukushima Nuclear Plant.
You ran away to shelters here and there with nothing but the clothes on
your back.
(You cannot return to your home as things stand.)

After four months, you could visit the house you had worried about for
so long,
only to find it had not flown away, was not broken, but was deserted.
Cherries, chestnuts, cucumbers, onions, ginger in the garden,
the familiar forests and river banks—
are all polluted by invisible radiation.
Your hometown is frozen in time.

In a panic, you hurriedly
put into your black bag
a dust mask, raincoat, white gloves, this and that . . .
Albums and sewing needles were abandoned, but the Buddhist
memorial tablet was not . . .
(You couldn't help leaving with regret . . . your hometown.)

Brought up by numerous folktales . . . born and raised . . . ,
for 78 years your hometown smiled and shed tears on you . . .
(It always watched over you and encouraged you . . . your hometown.)

You have lived in refugee camps—how many now?
You never leave the angry black plastic bag, not even for a moment.
You talk to your old friends who now live in different places.
You raise the black plastic bag high in the air, your act of defiance
against the "nuclear village."

Translated by Yorifumi Yaguchi

Tsutomu Sakai (1946-) Born in Nagano. Lives in Saku, Nagano.

THE POLLUTION OF OUR ANCESTRAL LAND

We picked edible wild plants in spring
and mushrooms in autumn.
But now *it* has approached
our mountains.

We can neither see *it*, nor hear *it*,
and *it* does not make any sound.

It comes suddenly on the wind,
falling on the earth,
infiltrating the soil in a flash,
lurking beneath the feet of animals,
the foretaste of an opaque death.

The mountains of our ancestral land are mourning.
Their angry voices ripple through the trees.
Leaves fall on the earth and sink in the water
accompanied by the melody of a *koto.*

Our ancestral land will become a wasteland.
These mountains will refuse even woodsmen,
now that no one is taking care of them.

Without saying anything,
these mountains cut a scar into the page of our future.
This demands a reply
from us haughty humans:

What in the world
have you done?

Translated by Yorifumi Yaguchi

__Akira Kijima__ (1962-) Born in Kanagawa. Lives in Yokohama, Kanagawa.

OUR HOUSEDOG WAS WATCHING US

The ground of Fukushima is
reflected in its moist beige eyes,
though people see only barren land in them.
Domesticated animals were let loose in the fields.
They calmly run around there kicking up the ashes of death.

For ten years or a hundred years
these fields will keep refusing humans.

Dogs once seen on remote surveillance cameras
have disappeared from those areas.
Their genes of obedience were cut off by the radiation.
Will they revert to the blood of wolves that they had long ago
forgotten?

For a thousand years, or for ten thousand years,
their cellular divisions will continue.

What kind of evolution will these animals undergo
as a result of the radiation?
And in what kind of world will they live?
Will there be a place for people?
Dogs accompanied by cows, pigs, and horses
raise their voices together in a battle cry
on the roofs of the deserted reactor buildings.

Awakened by this nightmare,
I find my housedog watching me.
Was it listening to the cries of the pack coming from a distant future?
In its moist eyes I found myself getting lost.

Translated by Yorifumi Yaguchi

Shouji Mitsui (1944-) Born in Yamagata. Lives in Yachiyo, Chiba.

A DIFFERENT VERSION OF "A RECORD OF THE LIVING"

Inside the 20-kilometer radius of the Fukushima No.1 Nuclear Power
Plant,
the radiation counter's needle now and then swings past the maximum.
People ran away with nothing but the clothes they wore.
Their pets became wild cats and wild dogs.
Cows and pigs were locked in and starved to death.
Maggots crawled through the skin and bones that remained.
Those that survived were slaughtered.
The wildlife—animals that escaped death in a ditch—ran free in the
irradiated environment.
Calves were born to cows that are no longer someone's livestock.
Packs of boars devastated the region in all directions.

Six kilometers from the stricken nuclear power station,
ostriches had been raised, bred carefully on only a small amount of food.
They were brought there to help the area prosper.
They were the symbol of the nuclear power station
that produced a great amount of electricity from a small amount of fuel.
Their skin became bags and belts,
their eggs became cookies and cakes,
and their meat tasted exotic.
Thus they became a tourist resource as domesticated animals.
They couldn't thrive in the cold and high humidity,
but they became mascots for the peaceful use of nuclear power.
Out of 30 birds, only a few survived, including the leader.
They were running around excitedly in the exclusion zone
as if they were in Africa, their ancestral home.
They survived for about a year before being deemed dangerous animals.
Six were caught in a culling operation, and as a consequence,
were used for research to study the effects of radiation.

Slogans dance vainly in the ghost towns:
A rich life with a proper understanding of nuclear energy.
The development of an atomic town and a prosperous future.
Signs still hang on shops in the ghost towns:
Atom for a daily-fresh conveyer belt sushi shop,
Atom for a pachinko parlor," and
Atomic Transportation for an electric supply company. . .

The animals sacrificed for the nuclear power stations
are symbols of us adults living today, and of our children in the future.

Translated by Yorifumi Yaguchi

Sumio Yukinaka (1938-) Born in Kyoto. Lives in Tenri, Nara.

A VISIT TO A NUCLEAR POWER STATION

Pearl Beach. We could see the power station we were heading toward
beyond the beautiful sea.
White cloud-like steam was billowing out
of the white cylindrical building.
Our car approached the station
on the road curving around the small bay.
From the drainage pipe, coffee-like water gushed out, bubbling all around.

The chief of the publicity department explained to us the mechanics
of the power plant
like a practiced speaker
emphasizing nuclear energy is easy on the earth,
gentle and safe. It does not produce CO2.

Question: *I saw white steam coming from the plant. Are you sure there is no radiation leaking?*
Answer: *I can't say there is absolutely no radiation, but there is no immediate effect on human health.*
Question: *The water from the drainage pipe is all brown. Is that all right?*
Answer: *There is no immediate effect on human health. The water was used only to cool down the atomic reactor.*
His explanation was correct and clear. He was smiling.

Toward the end of the tour, I raised my hand.
My question: *Do you eat the fish caught here in this sea at your own house?*
Answer: *No, we don't eat them at home.*
My question: *Do your children swim here on this beach?*
Answer: *No. I won't let them swim here.*
His answers were clear and precise.

More than twenty years have passed since that tour
to the place known as the Ginza of nuclear power stations—
the fish of Wakasa and the sea of Wakasa.
I think about that tour occasionally.

Translated by Yorifumi Yaguchi

Keiichiro Fujitani (1947-) Born in Ehime. Lives in Toyonaka, Osaka.

SWINDLING OF ONE MILLION YEARS

Healthy fingers and
dreaming hands

extend toward the expanding meadow of
dandelions and lotus

as if to grasp the blue sky,
and touch eternity.

*

But we,
though healed by such a routine,

have tended to step out
or be driven out
of the shadow of eternity.

Those who transplanted
the genes of the sun to this planet!
Those who shoot arrows to the sun
from this tower of Babel!

For the sake of your prosperity
of the next several decades,
haven't you swindled one million years
from the Japanese archipelago?

Weren't they
your skills, structures, capital and politics,
that could not respond
to an unforeseen once-in-a-thousand-year earthquake,
which caused the spread of high-level nuclear waste
when an unforeseen once-in-a-million-year movement of the earth's crust occurred?
At the moment of the hydrogen explosion at Fukushima No.1 Nuclear Power Plant,
the plaster of the walls floated up and stuck to the blue sky
as if it had been broken and fallen down.
It seemed to me as if the face of eternity became distorted
and disappeared.

*

The winds of prayer
blow quietly
through the Japanese archipelago
from the north and the west

in our heart, and

on the wordless field of life
of nuclear contamination
where the dandelions and the lotus spread.

Translated by Yorifumi Yaguchi

Rira Mizuki (1963-) Born in Kyoto. Lives in Maizuru, Kyoto.

THE TEN MILLION DOLLAR NIGHT VIEW

The big city is a
clear
dry jewel
yearning to be dazzled.

The brilliant lights
suited the darkness
too well.

In the gigantic boiling pots
standing along the beach
of the depopulated area,
uranium boils
and produces radiation.
It has been supporting a gorgeous paradise
of tens of millions of lights.
It was smiling
like a gentle spring that secretly turned into poison
and was thrown into the sea—
a sea of night in which fish with strange shapes swim.
The shadow of the moon floating on the mirror of the water
is asking for
something to happen without a lie.
A faint cry from the depths of the sea,
a gasp of the dream of the foreknowledge
of the sound of the waves—
fear at the thought
of laying eggs.

The ten million dollar night view
is extremely beautiful
and consoles our drunken desire.
It shines brighter than the stars and the moon
and is foaming with radiation.
Nothing is heard.
This is the place where the memory of no man exists.
Under the flood of artificial lights
one cannot smile from the heart.

Translated by Yorifumi Yaguchi

Tomomasa Sugimoto (1932-) Born in Okayama. Lives in Akaiwa, Okayama.

A SONG FOR TOMORROW

On that day, March 11, 2011,
the devil suddenly emerged from the earthquake of Eastern Japan.
Till that day, the people living on this planet
believed that nuclear power was the light of dreams and sang its praises.
They thought it was a treasure that would bring eternal happiness
and admired it as if it were a rainbow.
But the big earthquake taught them severely
that they had been completely mistaken.
They played a requiem in deep sorrow for the many victims
and spoke words of consolation for the sufferings of those affected.
The nuclear plant brought an entirely new agony.
For no one on this planet had seen the true aspect and ominous behavior
of this monster that had thrown off its disguise.
It acted with invisible, evil hands,
making people worry about many strange phenomena.
People could not control this devil,
could not contain it in the cage of their technical knowledge and skill.
We should abandon our overconfidence in this uncertain cage
and immediately part ways with this devil.
This star, this earth we live on,
is a place to join hands with our friends and take the bitter with the sweet.
Let us open our eyes and look around.
We can see abundant nature,
the smile of the sun burning red, the water reflecting the blue sky and the clouds,
trees and grasses in the forest which are full of the voice of eternal life,
the voice of the wind floating like songs and whispers high and low,
the earth producing our daily food with its hands raised strongly,
the thought of magma gushing forth with hot, boiling ideas.
The earth loves the whole of life here
like a mother embracing her baby gently.
The sunshine, the hands of water and wind,
the color of fire hiding in the trees,
the thought of the earth,
to unite all these will surely become the light of hope to illuminate the future.
Now, let us start walking to open the door of knowledge with one heart.
Let us continue praying
in order that a peaceful life may return to the deserted areas as soon as possible,
and a new day will dawn when we can hear songs of praise, full of smiles.

Translated by Yorifumi Yaguchi

Masayuki Nemoto (1946-) Born in Fukushima. Lives in Soma, Fukushima.

MY HOME, NAMIEMACHI

When did Fukushima become "*Fukushima*"?
Fukushima, which is written with Chinese characters meaning Lucky Island,
is now written in katakana.*
I was born and raised in Fukushima.
In the place called Namiemachi in Futaba County.
It used to be a verdant town
with the sea and the mountains
and two beautiful rivers.
Why did we have to flee?
Answer me.
I liked Namiemachi.
I liked it more than anyone.
I went fishing when I was a child.
I caught birds.
I played in the mountains and the rivers.
I laid in the fields
and watched the floating clouds.
Everything was beautiful.
People had beautiful hearts.
They remained pure
even after they had grown up.
They had flowers for all four seasons,
and people were kindhearted.
My home, Namiemachi.
I must come back to this land
someday by all means.
Even if it means hobbling with a cane,
I must come back
to my home, Namiemachi.

Translated by Keiko Shimada

---

* A Japanese script used to write loanwords of foreign origin; in this case, to indicate the worldwide notoriety of Fukushima.

Setsuko Okubo (1948-) Born in Fukushima. Lives in Nerima, Tokyo.

TO MY HOME

Butterbur sprouts, five-leaf aralia, fatsia sprouts, bracken, and parsley.
When the mountains are ready
for the sprouting of plants,

the rice fields are dug, and the fields are cultivated,
calves are born,
horses are pastured,
and chickens lay eggs.
It's a season full of life.

In the fall
Ears of rice rustle.
The smell of rice heralds the harvest.

Our prime blessing is brought by the soil
that has been developed over time.
That is a way of life that has been inherited and guarded.

In a twinkle it vanished.
It was not the explosive power
of an uncontrollable nuclear power plant,
but an invisible and merciless thing—
life-taking radiation—
that contaminated my home.

We had to slaughter the cows that we had tenderly watched over.
We abandoned our racehorses that we had raised with the utmost care,
left our houses, fields, and livestock, and evacuated.
We drift from shelter to shelter as refugees.

I dream of the fields and the mountains of my home.

The entrance has been sealed off.
Spring has rolled around again.
Butterbur sprouts, five-leaf aralia, fatsia sprouts, bracken, and parsley.
They are waiting to be picked
on the desolate land.

Translated by Keiko Shimada

Shonai Haga (1933-) Born in Fukushima. Lives in Saitama.

FETAL ACTIVITY OF BLUE

A pregnant woman can hear
the blue voice
of the blue sky.
It breaks the window of the unborn.
It breaks that lone window.
It is looking for
the only position
appropriate for a precious being.

Blue is in heaven
and in the sea.
Holding the controls
to subdue the overflow of blue,
a pregnant woman
swims in the ocean trench of life,
and dives to a depth of 8,000 meters.
She makes sure of the tides
deep within her body.
Since departures are always blue,
she goes deep.

Within a vehicle,
a fetus awakens.
In that fetus awakens
another fetus—
one after another.
A pregnant woman
wraps the fetus
in a heavy mitten each time,
and watches the sky.

When the blue voice of
the blue sky
falls on the map of her breath,
a blue spell springs forth from the earth.
The blue of heaven
applies the makeup of prayers to the mitten.
The blue of the earth
ebbs and flows,
slipping out of time.

Translated by Keiko Shimada

Hiroshi Suzuki (1958-) Born in Fukushima. Lives in Aizuwakamatsu, Fukushima.

DECONTAMINATION

We should dilute it
till it makes the radioactive contamination imperceptible.
We should wash it away.
We only need to get back the security of make-believe.

They eliminate the surface soil and wash the walls and roofs.
That is the disguise called decontamination.
Where can we flush away things
that will never become clean
in twenty thousand years?

They disregard people's sorrow and indignation in Fukushima.
Politicians forget their sense of mission
and just make unbelievable statements.
They never quit as politicians even after stepping down
from ministerial posts,
and just devote themselves to their party and personal interests.

Despite the fact that nuclear power plants
caused a large-scale accident that scattered radiation,
no one has taken any real responsibility for it.

Is this the ideal future for which young loyalists bled
at the risk of their own lives
only a hundred-some years ago?

The day when we can go home will not come soon
no matter how much contamination we wash and remove.
Who will wash away our sadness
of not being able to go home?

Where does the real dirt lie?
What should be decontaminated?
I hear the lamentations of samurai.

We see swindlers everywhere.
Only our courage to stand up to them
can begin to decontaminate the real dirt.

Translated by Keiko Shimada

Takao Ota (1937-) Born in Fukushima. Lives in Fukushima.

LIFE IS A TRUE TREASURE

Certainly it had been a rich coast and a rich sea unique to Japan.
The mountains were mantled in the luxuriant green of beech, oak, pine and chestnut trees.
People had wisely woven their daily routines into tranquil lives.

The war was over, and we got back the peace for which we had yearned and lit a fire of compassion.
From the Sanriku coast to Iwaki, and along the 500-kilometer coast of Ibaraki,
over sixty years of compassion was destroyed, broken, and swept away by the 9.0-magnitude earthquake.

We had rejected nuclear weapons
because of the atomic bombs and the radioactive damage to Hiroshima, Nagasaki and the Daigo Fukuryu Maru,
yet were dazzled by and accepted the magic of *peaceful utilization.*

Government and business firms working together in efficient partnership made use of the cheerful name of Fukushima
and continued constructing nuclear power plants.
A large tsunami swept aside four reactor buildings and the fictitious *myth of security.*
That radioactive materials were dispersed by the hydrogen explosions is a source of bitter regret.

People don't live simply in order to lose everything.
They enjoy the enveloping morning light and exchange words under starry skies.
Life is a true treasure,
their burning souls cry out
and they live on, with this expression ingrained in their hearts.

Chieko Takamura said, *The sky above Mt. Adatara is the true sky.*
In the land of cheerful Fukushima Prefecture, with its vast Lake Inawashiro,
people from the elderly to infants have no clean air to breathe
due to contamination by the colorless and odorless radiation.

The children unable to evacuate cannot enjoy sports festivals,
nor can they splash in swimming pools in the summer.
It is sad that they cannot go to the cicada-shrilling groves beyond the sunflower garden.

Translated by Keiko Shimada

Tamiko Kido (1959-) Born in Fukushima. Lives in Nihonmatsu, Fukushima.

FAIRYLAND

The land where I was born no longer exists.
Beyond it flutters a green wind.
It is a quiet place carpeted with rape blossoms,
filled with a hundred thousand years of sunshine.
A lovely breeze touches my cheek.

The sea where I was born no longer exists.
Waves shine, filled with the smell of the ocean.
Silver fish jump and flash in this calm and deep place.
Fine sand touches my toes.
The sea is still there, however.

Since that day in spring,
dreams have continued everywhere.
The sky, as well as the sea, changed their color.
It is the color of a scarlet lotus,
a color that halts the future.
It is a color that spreads out and announces itself to those left behind
in a dream.
This sorrow is the kind of sorrow that even sorrow cannot catch up with.

Heroes and saviors are here only temporarily.
There are lonely men too distraught to do anything
here and there.
It happened on a blue globe floating in the vacuous darkness.
It just happened.
I don't want to ascribe it to anyone,
nor to anything,
not even to nature.

The land where I was born no longer exists.
The sea where I was born no longer exists.
Beyond it flutters a green wind.
Waves shine, filled with the smell of the ocean.
They are not here, but they are there.
I'll go back there.
I'll go back there tomorrow.
I'll surely go back
to the land where I was born,
to the sea where I was born.

Translated by Keiko Shimada

Chihiro Uozumi (1944-) Born in Fukushima. Lives in Kanazawa, Ishikawa.

THE PLACE WHERE THE SOUL FLIES

There was a broad sky.
There was a deep blue sea.
A snowy white sand hill spread out, and deep green pinewoods grew thick.
The place where I was born and raised
was a quiet coastal town,
a place where the soul flies.

On that day,
Was it a cry or a scream of excess?
Human beings made nuclear power,
but human beings cannot control it.
That place was destroyed and broken
by a terrible gyration of nature.

No more.
Bearing the heavy burnt memory
of Hiroshima
and Nagasaki,
the Japanese archipelago has made its way for 65 years,
praying and yearning for peace.
That path
terminated in the sea at Fukushima,
and brutally exploded.

Imperishable material
blew away fantasy and myth in an instant.
Having no sound, no shape, no shadow,
it continues falling even today
and flows into tomorrow.
Is this a dream?
Is this peace?

There was a broad sky.
There was a deep blue sea.
My hometown
is still the place
to which my soul returns.

Translated by Keiko Shimada

Yasunari Kizuka (1954-) Born in Hiroshima. Lives in Kure, Hiroshima.

WASH

Not here any more is
the child who carries this satchel
even though his name is written on it.
His baseball cap was proudly torn
when it was finally dug up out of mud.
His mother, having neither thread nor needle,
washed the cap in the frigid stream, uttering,
Sorry, Dear, her hands turning red from the cold.

In the mud
are buried many promises not yet fulfilled:
dishes which must have been set on a table,
a still valid commuter pass,
a brand-new school uniform.
There are many more unfinished hopes.
This is some unknown family's album.
Those who closed it for the last time
must be cuddled close together somewhere unhurt.
And
I wish to place one more picture in the collage.
There should be another loving family here.
Photos covered in mud will be glossy again
washed by the hands of others those in the photos never knew.

That day the ocean was as brutal as anyone had ever seen.
The brown land shorn bare of trees,
footprints of sorrow everywhere increasing,
the howling of abandoned dogs
becoming louder day by day.
Now a gentle wind filled with rain
blows in from the calm sea
as if to wash the dirt from our brows.
You see, water doesn't do anything wrong.
It's our fault that we cannot stop the dark currents from swelling.
The beat of the rain only becomes more intense.

Translated by Junko Kimura

Hiromi Asayama (1954-) Born in Kyoto. Lives in Kyoto.

THE BEAUTIFUL FUTURE

For the lovely children
of the future,
now,
we have to put out
the nuclear fire,
or it will keep burning forever,
for there is no other way
no other path to take,
seeing our deserted hometown in front of us.

For the promising children
of the future,
now,
we must pledge
that suffering such as at Fukushima will be no more
on this planet.
Never again
will we see our hometowns brought to such misery
one after another, as we do now.
Thoughtful countrymen,
make a promise never to pollute with black rain
our mountains, streams, forests and fields,
where Japanese people used to feel
the Buddha's mercy.

I will pray
again and again,
that the children
of the future
will be able to collect colorful shells
washed ashore from far-away oceans.
After a hundred years,
may the children of the future,
here, in our hometown,
enjoy days more beautiful than these we now live through.

Translated by Junko Kimura

Akito Kitahara (1983-) Born in Tokyo. Lives in Edogawa, Tokyo.

THE HEARTBEAT

Some say that we still have time.
Some burst into tears saying it's too late.
Some complacently say that there's no problem that needs to be solved right away.
Each has his own reason, but something important is being overlooked.

If we say nothing, covering our eyes,
the reason for us to be here disappears.

Can we hear the sound of the world collapsing?
Can we hear the voices of living things in decline?
Can we hear? Do the sounds reach us?

How can we look them in the face—
all those who are approaching their end,
all those who are dying,
all the children who should have had a long future before them,
all those people living life just as they are. . .
What excuses do we have?
We, who can tell today from tomorrow,
are duty-bound to give an answer.

Before becoming a grain of sleeping sand,
we have only to keep going
in the direction that this heartbeat leads.
Along the path our soul beckons us,
before we are filled with grief and despair.

Our way back
will surely be recorded.

Translated by Junko Kimura

Jun Nakamura (1970-) Born in Tokyo. Lives in Kyoto.

TO THE NEW GENERATIONS

To the new generations

We have to apologize to you
for having deprived you of
the ground where you would have been able to walk barefoot,
the snowy fields into which you might have plunged with abandon,
the shallow brooks you could have splashed through,
the woods where you might have enjoyed sunbeams through the leaves,
colorful piles of fallen leaves,
crops safe and full of energy from the earth.

We have to apologize to you
for having exchanged lovely days for dirty money,
because of our ignorance, lack of awareness and stupidity,
for the lies of the gorgeous illuminations we conveyed,
for conveniences of life that you can control with a finger,
for a delicious lunch emitting 490 Bq of cesium,
for beautifully dished up dinners of genetically modified ingredients.

We have to apologize to you
for your damaged genes,
for the cesium detected in your body,
for your swollen thyroid gland.

What we can do now is to keep searching for
the truth, giving our warnings,
fighting on, fleeing together,
checking and selecting vegetables, meat and fish,
reconstructing our daily life with our own hands.

Let's start again from the beginning, from the very first day
when the ocean was still clean,
the soil was still fresh,
without forgetting the day that we human beings made a big mistake,
the day the nuclear power plant began walking toward
all mothers' wombs, toward the origin of life.

Translated by Junko Kimura

Junko Kimura (1936-) Born in Hokkaido. Lives in Sapporo, Hokkaido .

OH, HOW I WISH TO HAVE A FULL-BLOOMING CHERRY TREE

Oh, how I wish to have a full-blooming cherry tree
here, in the center of
this icebound white plain!

Its frozen heart stolen
by the faint smell of
full-blooming blossoms,
will the icy field forget its pride,
slowly loosening itself and
melt down?

When pink petals fall in a breeze
slight as a girl's sigh,
will the plain masked in white
slowly melt away,
its face now flushed,
losing self-control?

I wish to have a full-blooming cherry tree!
My numbed heart would be at ease
covered by swirls of falling petals.

Neither with radioactive snow,
nor with atomic black rain,
but only with profusely falling petals
will the sky warm the earth.
Only with a rain of pink petals
will the split and severed earth be healed.

Linking the heavens and the earth—

Oh, how I wish to have a full-blooming cherry tree
in the center of this icy white plain!

Translated by Junko Kimura

Kazuko Sanada (1952-) Born in Shimane. Lives in Takashima, Shiga.

TO TELL YOU THE TRUTH

I hate it
not being able to go back to my hometown

I hate it
being threatened by invisible things

I hate it
scolding children who want to play outdoors

I hate it
wearing a dosimeter round my neck

I hate it
losing touch with the people of my town

I hate it
robbing children of their future

I hate it
when water birds come in autumn
and eat water plants, unknowingly

I hate it
not being able to cook delicious fish from the lake

I hate it
if the lovely view of Lake Biwa would become only a memory*

I hate it
when the beautiful land is lost

I hate it
the monster that is nuclear power

I hate it

Translated by Eriya Tanase

---

* Two nuclear reactors are located in Tsuruga, near Lake Biwa. If a nuclear accident were to occur, the lake and its environs would be contaminated.

Koichi Omura (1961-) Born in Shizuoka. Lives in Shizuoka.

STEALTH

In the destroyed city,
a form clad in white
is reflected in the cracked and warped mirror as it passes by.
Its body is shattered, its parts disconnected.
The left side of its face in stark contrast to the right.

Almost everything is reflected as a shattered image.
In other words, the mirror shows almost nothing,
or should I say, everything is invisible.
Its face is invisible, hidden from everyone.
This is how my body, my reflection,
is projected in this world now.

Never will I live with a clear conscience.
The big doubt lies over everyone, contaminating them.
No one knows where to look for answers.
We are looking only for a rehash of yesterday's joys.
Whoever tries to deceive, or however I try to deceive myself,
we already know
that in the world we contaminated with our own hands,
my shattered image will never be restored,
that the shadow of death hangs heavy on everyone's back.

Translated by Eriya Tanase

Shinsuke Kusaka (1929-) Born in Fukui. Lives in Sapporo, Hokkaido.

AT TOMARI NUCLEAR PLANT

As I walk down the road
not far from the nuclear plant
children in bathing suits are playing on Horikappu Beach.

Having finished our visit to Tomarinkan*
we stand on the mountain top
looking down at the plant
on the shores of the deep-blue Sea of Japan,
Tomari Nuclear Plant with its cutting edge technology
and its grotesque reactor buildings
and groups of warehouses
storing containers of radioactive wastewater.

In the bay, a stone's throw away,
children are playing in the waves
on Iwanai Beach.

Remember Hiroshima and Nagasaki,
or the H-bomb tests in the atolls of Bikini,
all remote history for these children.

Eighteen years ago this sea** was stricken by the Okushiri Earthquake.
This year, on March 11, the Great East Japan Earthquake struck.
Nature convulsed, bringing the earthquake and tsunami,
and then the meltdown at the nuclear plant.

We have forgotten all of them—
the fact that beneath the rich fishing grounds and farmlands
the Earth's crust moves as it is destined,
the fact that in our short history Three Mile Island and Chernobyl
occurred.
The *Myth of Safety* has been disseminated in exchange for billions of yen
in subsidies.

We are all responsible for building nuclear plants,
cry out the children of Tokyo Electric Power Company workers
whose parents are criticized.

---

* Tomarinkan is the name of the nuclear power PR center for Hokkaido Electric.

** "This sea" refers to the Sea of Japan, on the western coast of Honshu.

The future of nuclear plants in Japan is caught up in the power struggle
of politicians who turn a deaf ear to the heated public debate.

Tomari Nuclear Plant glitters in the summer sunlight
but someday the radiation will get out of control.
Please don't let it destroy children's dreams!

Translated by Eriya Tanase

Ken Yamaguchi (1932-) Born in Yamaguchi. Lives in Karatsu, Saga.

YOU'RE GONNA GET IT!

The Japanese archipelago,
completely surrounded with fifty-four nuclear plants,
is like a prison in the ocean
isolating the prisoners.

The evil spirits in the jungles of the Nuclear Village*
have sent out messages of a Safety Myth with their Trojan Horse
utilizing narcotic nuclear plant money.

March 11, 2011, the Fukushima Nuclear Plant 1 had a hydrogen explosion,
releasing 168 times more radiation** than the Hiroshima Bomb,
and the reactor had a meltdown.

The deceivers in the Nuclear Village have all along continued to conceal
the whole picture,
chanting the spells of the Safety Myth,
and are now planning the con job, the restart.

You, who have sold your souls,
the people are boiling with rage!

August 15, 1945, we lost the war.
The Myth of Invincibility of the totalitarian emperor system collapsed.
You, who are trying to follow a fallen path,

You're gonna get it!

Translated by Eriya Tanase

* Special interest community of nuclear plant money and nuclear plant concessions.

** The release of cesium 137.

Shinobu Komura (1943-) Born in Palau. Lives in Izumi, Kagoshima.

THE DARKNESS OF BUILDING MORE NUCLEAR PLANTS

Oh, darkness of the great tsunami and the nuclear plants—
give us back our parents, our children
give us back the people, our homes,
our loves, our laughter.

Oh, anguished people, the more than 15,000 who lost their lives,
and the victims of the Fukushima nuclear plant accident,
Oh, sorrowful people who barely survived,
Oh, cruel deep darkness that freezes words:
see the lamentations and pain of people and all living things.

Born of nuclear plants, which they said were safe,
the stamens of Japanese cherry blossoms become torn petals,
or produce four petals instead of the normal five.
Deformities and large-scale death
of turtles and fish in the sea.
Why not unite the wisdom of Japan and the world?

Nuclear energy has already brought death and hell
to hundreds of thousands of people in Hiroshima and Nagasaki.
Why do they have to build more nuclear plants, using the same terrible
    energy?
And now they are at it again, planning to build the third Sendai
    Nuclear Plant.

Translated by Eriya Tanase

Hideko Yokota (1939-) Born in Osaka. Lives in Sakai, Osaka.

THE REVIVED PIANO

The broken sounds,
covered with mud, writhe and groan.
The legs of the piano, lid and keys
were scattered here and there
and buried—
in resentment against destruction.

The people lamented over
the sorry pieces and
made a vow to the blue sky.

With prayer, picking up the pieces
one by one from the mud,
they put them together
as if completing a puzzle.

At the site where once stood a musical instrument shop,
the love for the piano unfolded.
Not just that love,
but that the days before the destruction might be regained.
Let's reply to such a great deal of sorrow
and the voices now vanished.

The melodies
of the revived piano
are heard beyond the rumbling of the sea—
carried on the winds
beyond the horizon,
and from flocks of seagulls
are delivered to the people on the street.

From the orange waves
of drifting safflowers,
a joyous concerto—

This is the site where they dug the piano
out of the deep mud,
accompanied by
cheerful voices.

(inspired by the TV news of the day)

Translated by Aya Yuhki

Kenichi Saso (1968-) Born in Kanagawa. Lives in Shinjuku, Tokyo.

THE SOUND OF WAVES X

While I am absorbed in living,
time disappears.

While I am feeling tired or bitter,
I stumble in the sands of time.

While I stand listening to the sound of the waves,
the hands of the clock start moving backward
and a mirage pursues me—
I wish I had done
this or that.

But as I put my palm on my heart,
I feel I am surely alive.

Standing by the sea,
I look up at the sky full of sunshine.

Mercury, Venus, Mars, Jupiter, Saturn, Moon and Sun—
Earth ought to be the third planet of the solar system.
The life of the ancients—
without clocks, everyday they watched the sun and the moon,
listened to the voices of the wind and rain,
gazed at the sea, standing on the soil,
managed to get food,
build homes, make clothing,
and love each other.

Unnoticed wars expanded
unnoticed the gap between rich and poor enlarged
unnoticed the relationship of ruler and ruled grew apparent
unnoticed the hara-kiri
unnoticed the wars of aggression
unnoticed the World Wars
unnoticed the Cold War between East and West
unnoticed the American military bases in Japan
unnoticed the race for globalization
unnoticed the revision of history textbooks
unnoticed the dispatch of Self-Defense Force troops abroad

unnoticed the forest of nuclear reactors
unnoticed the commercialism
unnoticed the young men in the 100-yen shops
unnoticed the 21st century
Radiation and social inequality.

I touch my own body—
hands, legs, chest, belly, hips, back, face, nose, mouth, eyes and hair.
These days, I am conscious of my internal body—
I know my stomach, liver, pancreas, kidneys, heart, brain, veins and bones,
and, far deeper, a sense of *mind*.

The body of an anonymous poet in the *Manyoshu*
and that of a Cro-Magnon in primitive Eurasia
are almost the same as mine.

The mind—
has it evolved?

Digital watches, once very popular, are now out of date.
Looking at my simple wristwatch, the hands move toward the future.
Look! This planet also moves
around the sun.

Tonight is it possible to see the moon?
And tomorrow will the sun shine for us?

Telling myself, again and again, *I have not enough time,*
I stand by the sea at sunset—

YOU HAVE ENOUGH TIME
YOU CAN DO WHAT YOU NEED TO DO.

YOU MUST LIVE

I hear the sound of the waves anew.

Translated by Aya Yuhki

Megumi Watanabe (1965-) Born in Tokyo. Lives in Setagaya, Tokyo.

RESTART

The weather of peace is cloudy today.
The weather of poverty is fine today.
Within the embankment of justice
the shadows of people who have disappeared are dancing.
In the sanctuary
flowers will soon bloom.
The shadows increase one by one.
Some are crying,
their heads drooping,
over the value of what has been lost.
Everyone thinks,
It's all right. It couldn't be helped.
Thinking, *Spring will come, so we shouldn't cry,*
everyone falls asleep.
The seasons advance little by little,
and dreams develop
as precariously as the white of an egg.

How many angels did you see?
How did you know they were angels?
How did you know they were not betraying you?

With his back against the thick cold concrete wall,
the doctor keeps asking.

I can't answer. No, I can't.

Let us look, you and me, for an angel worthy of our trust.
Otherwise, the composition of the gene will be affected.

Inserting ova
into the vessel of February,
the determined woman closes her eyes.

(First appeared in *Shi no Hakken* No.11)

Translated by Naoshi Koriyama

Kazuko Shimomura (1932-) Born in Hyogo. Lives in Osaka.

LET'S LISTEN TO THE VOICELESS VOICE

The Jomon cedar can survive for 7,000 years
because of the deep darkness of the distant mountains.
In the Yakushima mountains at night
it is too dark for us to walk or to see even an inch in front of us.
As the King of the Forest, this tree stands guard.
I started early in the morning carrying two meals with me
and approached the tree after a ten hour walk in silence.
The days begin with ascent of the sun and end with decent of the sun.

If an alien from an unknown star were to come to investigate the earth,
he could probably not find it at night.
Trees also sleep at night.
Darkness gives trees and living creatures abundant sleep.
The sun is God.
In the sunlight, the sea, mountains, trees and human beings
used to live peacefully, each in harmony.

Now, whether in daytime or at night, the earth is glittering, dazzling.
The sun has lost its position as God.
The roadside trees in Osaka are said to have an astonishingly short lifespan.

Oil and atomic power control the world.
The rules of the universe are broken.
We are intoxicated with the convenience of artificial civilization,
and then become frightened about what we have created.
The sea, unable to understand the situation,
groping for direction, howls and writhes.
Each essence of nature suffers and roils.

Statutes of the Buddha, supposed to light the darkness of our hearts,
having lost their way in the artificial illumination
of the all-too-brilliant light of science,
appear simply as art, having lost their Buddha nature.
Forgive all just as they are—
as the essence of the Buddha is compassion.

There is no way except to be aware
and to listen to the voice of the earth.

Translated by Aya Yuhki

Ayumu Katagiri (1947-) Born in Nagano. Lives in Matsumoto, Nagano.

THE FIRE IN HELL

Over the nuclear power plants, birds fly,
unpleasant clouds float in a cracked blue sky,
white waves frolic at the shoreline,
and unassuming creatures continue on with their lives.
A labyrinth on the green field.
Birds suddenly fall from the sky and die,
and deformed frogs appear in the rice paddies,
but no one pays attention.
Although even the experts say
that the count is nothing to worry about,
the local people have been bathed
in high-count radiation.
Pregnant women and children, being highly susceptible,
have left the hometowns they loved.
When a hydrogen explosion shook the earth,
the river water became polluted with wormwood
and many people drank that water.
People experienced high fever and lost their lives
on the path to ruination.

Is it wise to operate
the ominous pots of Hell at this time?
They say they have automatic controls,
but there isn't anything as unreliable as this.
Imperfect humans are likely to make operational mistakes,
and there have been frequent minor accidents.
Radiation has leaked inside the buildings,
sometimes leading to internal exposure.
The operators lack precision and are careless.
Once lit, the fire will burn forever—
It is *God's Torch.*
Extinguishing the flame of bluish phosphorescence
is beyond human skill.
Burned uranium is separated into different elements,
scattered deadly ash mixes with the air,
sinks into the mud, and brings harm to life.
Before we know it, this invisible demonic material
comes to lodge in internal organs, destroys them,
and robs us of the fire of life.

Translated by Yuko Sawabe

Fumio Sato (1935-) Born in Tokyo. Lives in Sakura, Chiba.

THE HOLLOW EARTH

The Earth has been kicked up into the sky,
soars high
and is blown away to the edge of the galaxy.

What is the end that awaits the Earth?
What is waiting for the Earth in the deepest reaches of the galaxy?
Will it be the hell fire of a burning sun or a black hole?

Soon the Earth will collide with a huge group of meteorites.
The Earth will be kicked up again and soar even higher.
Between falling and being kicked up, being kicked up and falling,
the Earth will be entirely emptied of its contents.

With its contents gone, the hollow earth
will wander alone in the vast universe—
soaring and falling, falling and soaring.

As to the former inhabitants of the planet—
they were all shaken off and spilled out.
There is nothing, there is no one there any more.

The earth without anything, without anyone,
now wanders in the vast dark universe.

Translated by Yuko Sawabe

Akemi Fukumoto (1948-) Born in Kochi. Lives in Shimanto, Kochi.

BUDDING

Crops start bearing flowers, bush warblers begin to sing.
Wild rhododendrons and mountain cherries bloom.
Over this tranquil spring scenery, carried by the wind
the invisible threat of radiation descends.

Among those who opposed the nuclear power plant,
among those who supported the nuclear power plant,
as long as the fear remains embedded in the marrow of their bones,
March 11th won't be just any date, won't fade away.
We will speak about the nuclear accident for decades to come.
Before the radioactive contaminants leak out into the natural world,
we should recognize that this is not punishment from Heaven.

The season comes when insects begin to crawl,
but will they fall ill quietly and die?
Or will they evolve, adapting to the environment,
while waiting for things to settle down?

The season comes when we start building ridges to divide the rice paddies
that are our livelihood,
yet we cannot even welcome the God of the Rice Field.
Will people's feelings be conveyed to
the surviving animals, insects, butterflies and birds?

Since that day when we were suddenly severed from our homes,
and our eyes looked down in despair,
people have been laboring for restoration.
People who have become unperturbed by little things
will cherish the land, seeking the equilibrium of their souls.
We will not overlook the fact that
radiation is gnawing away at the branches growing out of control.

Before the Japanese archipelago becomes twisted and caves in,
crushed like a baby's hands by the upheavals of nature,
we should abolish nuclear power plants.

Let's enjoy the benefits of nature,
so that our lungs are infused with shades of green.
Spring comes around again without being arrogant.

May it continue eternally from now into the future.
With the pulsating flow of our blood, the depth of our prayers,
let's not forget what it was like this last March.

Translated by Yuko Sawabe

PAGE REFERENCES FOR THE POEMS

The poems that appear in *Reverberations from Fukushima: 50 Japanese Poets Speak Out,* edited by Leah Stenson and Asao Sarukawa Aroldi, published in 2014 by Inkwater Press, originally appeared in *Farewell Nuclear to Nuclear, Welcome to Renewable Energy: A Collection of Poems by 218 Poets,* published by Coal Sack Publishing Company in 2012 which was edited by Hisao Suzuki, Jotaro Wakamatsu, Yorifumi Yaguchi, Fumiko Suzuki, Hiromi Misho and Kenichi Saso and translated by Naoshi Koriyama, Yorifumi Yaguchi, Junko Kimura, Aya Yuhki, Keiko Shimada, Eriya Tanase and Yuko Sawabe. The following poems are listed according to the chapter and page on which they appeared in Coal Sack's publication. For further information regarding these poems or other titles published by Coal Sack Publishing Company, 2-63-4-509 Itabashi, Itabashi-ku, Tokyo (173-0004) Japan, please e-mail: Suzuki@coal-sack.com.

Chapter I—Catastrophes Foreseen

1. To Give Birth—Rumiko Kora, p.18-19
2. At the Night of Seeing the Summer Off—Fumiko Suzuki, p. 22-23
3. A Land of Sorrow: A City Spirited Away By God A Litany (6)—Jotaro Wakamatsu, p.28-29
4. The Site Where Dangerous Objects Are Buried—Mariko Fukuda, p. 30
5. Ventilation—Yukari Mutou, p. 32
6. A Letter From The Shroud—Hisao Suzuki, p. 33
7. The Walls—Kazunari Usuki, p. 37
8. If Man Snatches the Fire—Eiji Kuroha, p.38

Chapter II—The Repeated Mistake

1. What Should We Do?—Hiromi Mishou, p.45
2. Einstein's Voice—Hiroyoshi Komatsu, p. 46
3. Helen Keller's Fingertips—Masanori Shida, p. 52
4. Transition Of A Myth—Masumi Tanizaki, p. 55
5. Like Tomatoes—Shizuka Kawana, p. 57
6. A Phantom Country of Civilization—Ryu Nishina, p. 62
7. Give Us Back Everything—Yasunori Akiyama, p. 64

Chapter VII—Making Myths of Denuclearization

Nothing included

Chapter VIII—Voices from the Sea

1. Let's Listen To The Voiceless Voice—Kazuko Shimomura, p. 195
2. Restarting Nuclear Reactors—Megumi Watanabe, p. 197
3. The Revived Piano—Hideko Yokota, p. 198
4. The Sound of Waves X—Kenichi Saso, p. 214-215

Chapter IX—Petitions from the Sun and Moon

1. The Hollow Earth—Fumio Sato, p. 220
2. The Fire In Hell—Ayumu Katagiri, p. 235
3. Budding—Akemi Fukumoto, p. 237

Chapter X—Produce Electricity that Is Safe for Human Beings

Nothing included

Chapter XI—Poems for Fukushima from Poets Overseas

Nothing included

Bio of Leah Stenson

After graduating with an M.A. in English Literature from State University of New York at Stony Brook, Leah Stenson worked as an assistant editor in New York City for Hawthorne Books and School Library Journal. In 1977, she moved to Tokyo to pursue a spiritual quest to deepen her understanding of Buddhism and spent 16 years teaching English at a Japanese university and a women's junior College. In 1993 she moved to Portland, Oregon where she served for several years as the managing director of Oregon Peace Institute while continuing to do freelance editorial work. She is an actively practicing Buddhist and a member of the Interfaith Council of Greater Portland. She serves on the board of Friends of William Stafford and hosts the Studio Series, a monthly poetry reading and open mic.

Leah has published essays, editorials and feature articles for various newspapers and magazines and co-authored a textbook for Japanese students of English in addition to publishing poetry in literary journals and magazines. Her chapbook, *Heavenly Body*, was published by Finishing Line Press in 2011 and "The Turquoise Bee and Other Love Poems" is scheduled to be published by the same press in 2014. She served as a regional editor for *Alive at the Center: Contemporary Poems from the Pacific Northwest* (Ooligan Press, 2013)

For further information visit: www.leahstenson.com.

Bio of Asao Sarukawa Aroldi

Asao Sarukawa Aroldi was born in Tokyo. After graduating with a B.A. in art history from University of Leicester, and subsequently completing a Ph.D. in Japanese art history at University of East Anglia, she moved back to Tokyo where she worked at a publishing company and then at a translation agency. She now lives in Locarno, Switzerland where she works as a freelance translator.

"The cart that overturns on the road ahead is a warning to the one behind." – *Buddhist proverb*

福島からの反響音

――日本の詩人50人の発信

福島からの反響音

——日本の詩人50人の発信

リア・ステンソン　編
猿川アロルディ麻緒　編

序文

福島で原発事故があったことを知ったわたしは、まるでギリシャ悲劇を見ているかのような、にわかには信じがたい気持ちでそのニュースの一部始終を追っていた。わたしの暮らすアメリカ北西部の街は、放射能汚染の激しいハンフォード核施設から二〇〇マイル下流に位置している。ハンフォードといえば、長崎に投下された原子爆弾に使われたプルトニウムが製造された場所で、被曝はわたしにとって決して他人事とは思えない身近な恐怖である。福島で起きている大惨事の様子が明らかになるにつれ、放射性プルームが風に乗ってアメリカ西海岸に到達するのも時間の問題だということもわかってきた。福島原発の惨状にわたしは戦き、その経過をつぶさに注視した。

それから二年という歳月が流れるうちに、福島がニュースに取り上げられることもなくなり、世間の意識からすっかり遠のいてしまった。今も福島の人びとが苦しみ続けていることを大多数のアメリカ人は知らない。原発事故から四年目を迎える今、ウランを利用する原子力を取り巻く陰謀と放射能がもたらす悲劇を語る日本の詩人たちの声に耳を傾け、もう一度、福島に思いを馳せることはとても意義のあることだと考える。

本書『福島からの反響音——日本の詩人50人の発信』を出版する目的は二つある。

一つ目は、ウランを利用した原子力発電の甚大な危険性を、一般のアメリカ人に知らしめること。ウランをベースにした核エネルギーは、その強力さゆえに人類に計り知れない危険をもたらすことを私たちは認識しなければならない。

二つ目は、日本の現代詩に対する理解を深めること。これまで、俳句や短歌といった伝統的な詩の形態を除いては、アメリカで日本の詩が読まれることはほとんどなかった。日本の詩人による多彩な詩の表現を本書で紹介することで、日本の現代詩が多くのアメリカ人の目に触れ、その真価が認められることを願っている。

プロジェクトを始めてすぐに、アメリカにいながら福島をテーマに書かれた日本語の詩を探し出さなければならないという壁につきあたった。そんな中、本書の共同編集者である猿川アロルディ麻緒と知り合ったのは、幸運なことだった。彼女は3・11以降、脱原発への気運が高まる東京でデモに参加し、脱原発世界会議でボランティア活動をするなど、個人として原発問題について考え、行動に移してきたひとりだ。

彼女が『脱原発・自然エネルギー218人集』（鈴木比佐雄ほか編、コールサック社・二〇一二年）を見つけ出し、出版社に連絡を取ると、編集者の鈴木比佐雄氏は、詩選集をアメリカの読者に親しみやすいかたちに編集し出版することを即座

に快諾してくださった。

このような経緯で、本書はインクウォーター・プレス社から出版される運びとなった。50編の詩は、福島の惨状に対する怒りの表現である。これを読むものは、50人の詩人たちの情熱に満ちた力強い声を聞くだろう。その声はまた、何千、何万という福島の人びとの声を代弁するものである。人間と自然との間の均衡の回復を求める切実な訴えでもある。

これらの詩は、習わしや生命の循環を軽視した人間を待つ結末を、豊かな言葉でうたいあげる。そして福島を待つ運命を予見し、人びとのふるさとが、生活が失われた悲しみを描く。詩人たちは、人の命を食いものにするものとされるものが共に破滅のサイクルに絡めとられる悲劇を物語ると同時に、日本の一般市民がいかにして原子力の「公益」について洗脳されてきたかを語る。

本書の詩を読むことによって、福島で起きた原発事故が単に「災害」という無機質な言葉で片付けられるものではないこと、そして事故によってもたらされた計り知れないほどの苦しみを堪え忍んでいる人たちがいることを、アメリカの読者が心で感じ取ってくれることを願っている。

本書のベースとなった『脱原発・自然エネルギー218人集』から50編を再出版することを承諾してくださったコールサック社代表の鈴木比佐雄氏と出会えたことは非常に幸運だった。鈴木氏はまた、本書にも作品が含まれる、福島の詩人二人を紹介してくださった人でもある。そのうちの一人で、原発事故によって現在も避難を余儀なくされている根本昌幸氏は、詩「わが浪江町」で離れざるを得なかった故郷への愛着を切々とうたっている。根本氏の取り計らいにより、避難区域となっている浪江町を私は夫、娘と共に訪れることができた。

避難区域に指定された福島第一原発周辺の町々を実際に目にすることで、この地域の状況に対する理解を深めることができたと思っている。それでも、この体験は私にとってあまりにも生々しく、福島で起こっている悲劇の規模やその意味するところをいまだに把握しかねているというのも事実だ。福島県のうち、五〇〇平方マイルにあたる地域に人が住めなくなってしまったということ。今でもおよそ十五万人にのぼる人びとが避難を余儀なくされているということ。そしてそれらの多くの人たちは、死ぬまでふるさとに帰ることができないかもしれないということ。

地震や津波による直接の被害を受けなかったにも関わらず人が住めなくなってしまったゴーストタウンは、まるで役者たちが去ったあとの映画のセットのようだった。家々や店が立ち並ぶ通りに、まるで人の気配がないということの不気味さは

筆舌に尽くしがたい。

鈴木氏が紹介してくださった二人目の詩人、若松丈太郎氏に出会えたこともとても幸運なことだった。若松氏は一部が警戒区域とされた南相馬市に暮らし、福島第二原発設置許可取り消し訴訟の原告として何十年も前から戦ってきた経緯を持つ活動家でもある。しかし原子力発電の危険を暴こうとする彼の努力は、原発が地域に経済的な利益をもたらすと信じる隣人たちにとっては受け入れがたいことだった。原発事故のあったチェルノブイリを訪れた若松氏は、本書にも取り上げる「連詩　かなしみの土地　6　神隠しされた街」を迫力のある筆致で書き上げた。この詩は、福島で起こる原発事故を鋭く予見していたのだが、若松氏や、反核を訴え共に戦ってきた鈴木比佐雄氏の予言的な言葉に耳を貸す人はほとんどいなかったという。

私はこれら三人の詩人たちに出会えたことを光栄に思うと同時に、彼らの精力的な反核活動に深い感銘を受けた。そして彼らが、本詩選集をアメリカで出版したいという私の気持ちを理解してくださったことを喜ばしく思う。日本国外で彼らの声を代弁する詩を紹介することで、日本政府から忘れ去られたと感じている福島の人たちを少しでも励ますことができたらこれ以上のことはない。

これらの詩人を私に紹介してくださり、本書の出版に惜しみない協力をしてくださった鈴木比佐雄氏に心から感謝を申し上げる。編集者の鈴木氏は、本詩選集の代表作でもある優れた詩「シュラウドからの手紙」を書いた詩人でもある。高い社会的意識と確固たる信念を持って原子力を批判し、核兵器の使用を糾弾する書籍を出版し続けている鈴木氏に敬意を表したい。

福島の詩人たちと連帯し、友情を結ぶことができたことで、私にとってこの詩選集の出版はさらに意義のあることとなった。それぞれの地域や国で私たちが人間性を保つことのできるよう結束することは、核のない安全な世界を実現するチャンスを高めることになると私は確信している。

私たちはみな同じ空の下に暮らしている。放射性プルームから逃げられる場所などない。福島がそうであったように、原子力発電所や核施設がある限り、想像を絶する被害をもたらす「予期せぬ事故」はいつでも起こりうる。次はアメリカかもしれない。世界のどこであろうと事故は起こりうるのだ。「前車のくつがへすは後車のいましめぞかし」とは仏教の言葉である。福島から学べるか否かは、私たちにかかっている。

オレゴン州ポートランドにて

リア・ステンソン

英訳の校正に関する注記

本書『福島からの反響音――日本の詩人50人の発信』を構成する50編の詩作品の英訳はもともと、日本に在住の日本人翻訳者が行い、コールサック社出版の『脱原発・自然エネルギー218人集』に掲載されたものです。

『脱原発・自然エネルギー218人集』の縮小版をアメリカで出版するにあたり、これらの作品をアメリカの読者にとって受け入れやすい形で紹介するためにも、私は元の英訳を再校正する必要があると考えました。翻訳が詩人の言葉に忠実でありながらも、英語の読みやすさと、アメリカ人には馴染みのない概念や日本文化の側面を的確に表現するものであるよう、最大限の努力を払いました。それでもこの校正作業は、決して容易いものではありませんでした。

『脱原発・自然エネルギー218人集』と本書を読み比べられる読者は、それぞれに掲載された詩作品50編の英訳が同一のものではないことに気がつかれると思います。私は十六年間日本に暮らし、日本語と日本文化に親しんできましたが、自分自身を翻訳者と呼べるほど日本語に通じている訳ではありません。むしろ、翻訳を引き立てることが私の編集者としての役目であると考えます。そのため、個々の作品のページには、英訳を行った日本人翻訳者の名前を記載しました。

コールサック社出版の『脱原発・自然エネルギー218人集』に掲載された詩作品のリストとそれらのページ番号については、「詩作品の出典」をご参照ください。

リア・ステンソン

詩　目次

シュラウドからの手紙

鈴木　比佐雄（すずき　ひさお）

1954年、東京都生れ。詩集『鈴木比佐雄詩選集一三三篇』、詩論集『詩人の深層探求』。詩誌「COAL　SACK」、日本現代詩人会所属。千葉県柏市に暮す。

父と母が生まれた福島の海辺に
いまも荒波は押し寄せているだろう
波は少年の私を海底の砂に巻き込み
塩水を呑ませ浜まで打ち上げていった

波はいま原発の温排水を冷まし続けているのか
人を狂気に駆らすものは何がきっかけだろうか
検査データを改ざんした日
その人は胸に痛みを覚えたはずだ
その人は嘘のために胸が張り裂けそうになって
シュラウド（炉心隔壁）のように熱疲労で
眠れなくなったかも知れない

二〇〇〇年七月
その人はシュラウドのひび割れが
もっと広がり張り裂けるのを恐怖した
東京電力が十年にわたって
ひび割れを改ざんしていたことを内部告発した
二年後の二〇〇二年八月　告発は事実と認められた
私はその人の胸の格闘（ひびわれ）を聞いてみたい
その良心的で英雄的な告発をたたえたい

そのような告発の風土が育たなければ
東北がチェルノブイリのように破壊される日が必ず来る
福島第一原発　六基
福島第二原発　四基
新潟柏崎刈羽原発　三基
十三基の中のひび割れた未修理の五基を
原子力・安全保安院と東京電力はいまだ運転を続けている
残り八基もどう考えてもあやしい

国家と電力会社は決して真実を語らない
組織は技術力のひび割れを隠し続ける
福島と新潟の海辺の民に
シュラウドからの手紙は今度いつ届くのだろうか
次の手紙ではシュラウドのひび割れが
老朽化した原発全体のひび割れになっていることを告げ
るか

子供のころ遊んだ福島の海辺にはまだ原発はなかった
あと何千年たったらそのころの海辺に戻れるのだろうか
未来の海辺には脱原発の記念碑にその人の名が刻まれ
その周りで子供たちが波とたわむれているだろうか

（初出・二〇〇二年）

壁

宇宿　一成（うすき　かずなり）
1961年、鹿児島県生れ。詩集『賑やかな眠り』『固い薔薇』『光のしっぽ』。詩人会議、日本現代詩人会、日本詩人クラブ所属。鹿児島県指宿市に暮す。

耐震のために岩盤に直接
原発の建屋は固定されているという
放射性物質を封じ込めるために
幾重にも壁をめぐらせて

しかし命がいつか
内包する死によって
完成するように
壁は必ずいつか
抱えているものによって
壊れるほかないのだろう
そのときはじめて
私たちは
幾重にもおおい隠していたものの
本当の顔に出会うのだ

＊初出・「詩と思想」二〇〇七年十月号

時ならぬ冷たさで
六月の雨が降っていた
狭いアパートで男が首を吊った
恋人に誓ったとおりに
君のために死ぬ、とファンタジーのような遺書を残して

悲劇は美しいと呟くのは
あなたが死を抱えた生であるから
生きることの中に
強く死を意識したから

頭蓋骨が脳を包み込むように
人は身体という壁で
死を包み込んでいて
それでもそこから漏れる
かすかな
死の匂いに飾られている

ウラン燃料の小さなペレットを
北薩の地盤が抱いている

火を奪えば

黒羽　英二（くろは　えいじ）
1931年、東京都生れ。詩集『遺跡』『鐵道癈線跡と』『移ろい』。日本現代詩人会、日本詩人クラブ、日本文藝家協会所属。神奈川県中郡に暮す。

天の崩れ落ちるのをおそれて
心いためたのは杞の国の人だったが
いま大磯東小磯清水のヤトに住んでいて
原子の時代もはや原始の時代に還れぬをかなしみ

太陽なる半径七〇万キロメートルの巨大火球
虚空に浮び
一千億気圧の超高圧をつくるため
一千五百万度の高温発し続ける姿を思う

火の神の手から秘密奪い取り
原子炉に低濃縮ウランを
原爆用には高濃縮ウランを使って
核分裂連鎖反応起させて巨大エネルギー生み出したが

ヒロシマには「チビ（リトルボーイ）」を
ナガサキには「デブ　（ファットマン）」を落して
一瞬のうちに数十万人の生命を奪っただけではなく
五年後までの死者は広島二十万長崎十四万人に達した

ウランやプルトニウム冷却材と反応するのを防ぐため
金属の皮膜かぶせて燃料に加工し
放射能閉じ込めるため
原子炉利用して核分裂起して燃料としたが

使用ずみ核燃料の中のウランとプルトニウム回収して
原子燃料再処理工場東海村に作り一九七七年試運転始め
電力供給にフル稼働のさ中チェルノブイリで大惨事起り
無限の恐怖　原子の時代もはや原始に還れぬ絶望告げる

ネヴァダ　ビキニ　カザフスタン　タクラマカン
スリーマイル　チェルノブイリ　X　Y　Z
海に潜り空を飛び宇宙へ飛び出して
利便追求止める術なきヒト絶滅の日迫るを知れば

（初出・二〇〇八年頃）

夏を送る夜に
――原発ジプシー逝く――

鈴木　文子（すずき　ふみこ）
1942年、千葉県生れ。詩集『女にさよなら』『鳳仙花』『電車道』。詩誌「炎樹」、詩人会議、日本現代詩人会所属。千葉県我孫子に暮す。

いいやつだったなあ。
ああ　いいやつだった。
それにしてもものんべえだったなあ。
のむしかなかったのよ。

百姓やめて何年んなる。
田畑(でんばた)くさぼうぼうんなって五年よ。
漁に出なくなって三年半。
不漁つづきで　借金かかえて、
どうにもなんなかった。
そんな時、
請負いの親方がきたってわけさ。
十分か二十分働いて、
たった三分で一日の手間もらったこともある。
命がけで魚とってたもんにとっちゃあ、
原発さまさまだった。

百姓だっておんなじよ。
なんにも知らねで、
ゴムのカッパ着て　長グツはいて、
宇宙人みてなマスクつけて、
マスクは苦しいからはずして仕事した。
いつだったか
炉の床にこぼれた水ふきとってたら、
胸に下げたアラーム・メーターが、
ビービー鳴ってうるせえのなんの。
そんなの無視して作業やったけんどな。

そらあそうだ。
メーターがパンクしたって
やめられるもんじゃねえ。
上のせ手当ほしかったもんな。
あしたっから仕事もらえなくなったら、
そのことばっかり考えて。
仕事終っと
一二〇ミリレムって
被曝基準*どおりに書いたもんだ。

二〇〇ミリレムこえると、
メーターの針が切れるそうだ。

放射能は、
見えるわけじゃなし　臭くもなし。
仕事してっとき、
どこかが痛くなることもなし、
恐ろしいなんて信じられねえんだな。
覚えてるかい　あの黒人のこと。
でっかい体で真っ白い歯で、
コニチワ。
日本語はコニチワとサヨナラだけで。
体でリズムとりながらペラペラしゃべって、
人なつこい気のよさそうな青年だった。
両手をいっぱいひろげて、
首をちょこんと曲げて、
サヨナラ。
ひび割れた炉ん中で、
一〇〇〇ミリレムもあびたって話だが、
無事に国へ帰れたろうか――。
若くて肌が光ってたから、
毒なんかしみなかっただろうよ。
きっと　そうしみなかった。

いいやつだったなあ。
ああ。
もうすぐおれたちも。

まぁ　一パイいこうか。
ああ……

＊レムは放射線量の単位（現在はシーベルト）。法律では五〇〇ミリレムと決まっているが、これはとんでもない主張。

＊初出「海風」創刊号・一九八七年・海風の会

危険物埋蔵地

原発事故がかすめた地域では
木いちごの実が摘めません
ジャムも作れないし
いま眼の前で跳びはねている
鳥やけものたちはすべて殺さなければなりません
それらはまとめられ暗い穴の中に埋められます
危険物埋蔵地――なんとウソさむい表示
地獄草子にもなかったことだ
春の花野の生命の場所が
いっせいに血を吹いて死に絶え
死んだばかりか怨念の復讐をつづけるのです
危険物埋蔵地
もう森へははいれません
野あそびでこころを洗うこともできません
セシウムの花が咲く風の方向におびえ
行ったものは帰れません
行って帰ってこれないなんて
そんな馬鹿げたことを性こりもなく
にんげんがしているなんて
神さまにどうやって説明するの？

福田　万里子（ふくだ　まりこ）
1933〜2006年、東京都生れ。詩集『柿若葉のころ』『福田万里子全詩集』、エッセイ集『花ばなの譜』。詩誌「アルメ」「楽市」。佐賀県で育ち大阪府枚方市に暮した。

小さな女の子の眼がそういってます
ほんとうに
なんと説明するのでしょうねえ
感動とは
昔を記憶によみがえらせて
生命をつなぐことではなかったか

「五歳の子供がニュースを聴く。六歳はデモをし
七歳は砂、車、花（の汚染）を心配する」と西ドイ
ツの週刊誌「シュテルン」は伝えている*

小さな子供たちの小さな胸は
ほんの少しの幸福で一杯になるはずなのに
森や公園のかくし絵のような愉しさは皆無で
危険物埋蔵地――
激しくみえてくる表示の予感を
暗く波動させているばかりです
きょうの風はどこから吹いてくるのだろうか
もうお話は生まれません

*高木仁三郎『チェルノブイリ・最後の警告』より

（初出・一九九五年）

換気

武藤　ゆかり（むとう　ゆかり）

お爺ちゃん
窓を閉めてくださいね
近くの工場で事故があって
放射性物質が飛んでいるんですよ
ひひひ
看護婦さんよ
今日は暑いんだわ
換気だ換気
お爺ちゃん
開けたら危ないんですよ
公報で言っているのよ
ひひひ
だけど臭くてよ
あいつ漏らしたからよお
駄目ですって空気を吸っちゃ
どう言ったら分かるの
看護婦さんよ
何も飛んでねえぞ
ひひひ

1965年、茨城県生れ。詩集『仏の炎神の水』『水の一族』『月と日のあわいに』。
詩誌「COAL　SACK」、詩を語る会所属。茨城県那珂郡に暮す。

産む

高良　留美子（こうら　るみこ）
1932年、東京都生れ。詩集『崖下の道』『高良留美子詩集』。新・フェミニズム批評の会所属。東京都目黒区に暮す。

産むという漢字は
女が坐産*をしているところを表したものだ　と
聞いたことがあったかなかったか
原子力発電所の建った村に
わずかにのこされた産小屋で
年老いた女が
繰り返してきたお産を語る
天井からたれ下がった一本の力綱
砂の上に向きあうように積み上げられた
二十四個のわらの小束
女はそのわら束にもたれかかり
綱をつかんで　からだを浮かした
日本海の鈍色（にびいろ）の波が岸辺を打ち
降りかかる雪が海に消える
産道に似た道が　村を横切る
女たちはそうやって産み
産みつづけてきたのに
道はいつもあらぬ方角につづいていた
人は道に行き暮れ
分かれ分かれにされ　迷い
暗い渦に巻きこまれる
人は帰るところを失い
立ちつくす

産むという漢字のなかにある生という字は
生まれてきた赤んぼうを表したものだ　と
聞いたことがあったかなかったか
肛門のところをかかとで押すと
赤んぼうがうしろの方へいきたがるのが
ふせげるんだよ　と
海からだけ光のはいる産小屋で
四人の子を産んできた女は語る
小屋の前には細い川が流れていて
女はそこで米をとぎ　御飯を炊く

かつては産小屋を出る日
日本海の夜明けのなぎさで
波をかぶり　波をくぐった
死の世界から　甦るために

女はそうやって産み
産みつづけてきたのに　その産道は
ついに原子力発電所までつづいていたのか
道の行方を見きわめてこなかったために
道は産む者と産まれる者を分かち
人は日暮れた道を一人たどらねばならない
女の産む姿を　一個の漢字のなかに
凝固したまま

＊坐産（ざさん）＝坐った姿勢での伝統的なお産

「新日本文学」一九八三年一一～一二月合併号に発表。詩集『仮面の声』（土曜美術社）、『高良留美子詩集』（土曜美術社出版販売）、『命が危ない３１１人詩集』（コールサック社）に収録。

連詩　かなしみの土地　6
神隠しされた街

四万五千の人びとが二時間のあいだに消えた
サッカーゲームが終わって競技場から立ち去った
のではない
人びとの暮らしがひとつの都市からそっくり消えたのだ
ラジオで避難警報があって
「三日分の食料を準備してください」
多くの人は三日たてば帰れると思って
ちいさな手提げ袋をもって
なかには仔猫だけをだいた老婆も
入院加療中の病人も
千百台のバスに乗って
四万五千の人びとが二時間のあいだに消えた
鬼ごっこする子どもたちの歓声が
隣人との垣根ごしのあいさつが
郵便配達夫の自転車のベル音が
ボルシチを煮るにおいが
家々の窓の夜のあかりが
人びとの暮らしが
地図のうえからプリピャチ市が消えた
チェルノブイリ事故発生四〇時間後のことである
千百台のバスに乗って

若松　丈太郎（わかまつ　じょうたろう）
1935年、岩手県生れ。詩集『いくつもの川があって』『越境する霧』、エッセイ集『福島原発難民』。詩誌「新現代詩」「いのちの籠」「福島自由人」。福島県南相馬市に暮す。

プリピャチ市民が二時間のあいだにちりぢりに
近隣三村をあわせて四万九千人が消えた
四万九千人といえば
私の住む原町市の人口にひとしい
さらに
原子力発電所中心半径三〇kmゾーンは危険地帯とされ
十一日目の五月六日から三日のあいだに九万二千人が
あわせて約十五万人
人びとは一〇〇kmや一五〇km先の農村にちりぢりに消えた
半径三〇kmゾーンといえば
東京電力福島原子力発電所を中心に据えると
双葉町　大熊町　富岡町
楢葉町　浪江町　広野町
川内村　都路村　葛尾村
小高町　いわき市北部
そして私の住む原町市がふくまれる
こちらもあわせて約十五万人
私たちが消えるべき先はどこか
私たちはどこに姿を消せばいいのか
事故六年のちに避難命令が出た村さえもある
事故八年のちの旧プリピャチ市に

私たちは入った
亀裂がはいったペーヴメントの
ツバメが飛んでいる
ハトが胸をふくらませている
チョウが草花に羽をやすめている
ハエがおちつきなく動いている
蚊柱が回転している
街路樹の葉が風に身をゆだねている
それなのに
人声のしない都市
人の歩いていない都市
四万五千の人びとがかくれんぼしている都市
鬼の私は捜しまわる
幼稚園のホールに投げ捨てられた玩具
台所のこんろにかけられたシチュー鍋
オフィスの机上のひろげたままの書類
ついさっきまで人がいた気配はどこにもあるのに
日がもう暮れる
鬼の私はとほうに暮れる
友だちがみんな神隠しにあってしまって
私は広場にひとり立ちつくす
デパートもホテルも
文化会館も学校も
集合住宅も
崩れはじめている
すべてはほろびへと向かう
人びとのいのちと
人びとがつくった都市と
ほろびをきそいあう
ストロンチウム九〇　半減期　二七・七年
セシウム一三七　　半減期　　三〇年
プルトニウム二三九　半減期二四四〇〇年
セシウムの放射線量が八分の一に減るまでに九十年
致死量八倍のセシウムは九十年後も生きものを殺しつづ
ける
人は百年後のことに自分の手を下せないということであ
れば
人がプルトニウムを扱うのは不遜というべきか
捨てられた幼稚園の広場を歩く
雑草に踏み入れる
雑草に付着していた核種が舞いあがったにちがいない
肺は核種のまじった空気をとりこんだにちがいない
神隠しの街は地上にいっそうふえるにちがいない
私たちの神隠しはきょうかもしれない
うしろで子どもの声がした気がする
ふりむいてもだれもいない
なにかが背筋をぞくっと襲う
広場にひとり立ちつくす

（初出・一九九四年）

重い歳月

故郷の海岸線は原発の銀座になり
人々の素朴な暮しのありようも
人々の眼付きも
心なしか変わってしまった十年だった

私たちの一生も限りがあるから
誰にとっても十年は永かった
だが
慣れない金策に駆けまわり
署名を集め　勉強会もする
この十年がなかったら
私たちの人生はやせ細ったものになっただろう

それにしても空しい判決だった
空しさはどこから来るのか
裁判官が真実から眼をそむけたから
権力に尻尾を振ったから

空しいのは彼らであって
私たちではない

〈真実〉はいつも少数派だった
今の私たちのように

しかし原発はいつの日か
かならず人間に牙をむく
この猛獣を
曇りない視線で監視するのが私たちだ
この怪物を絶えず否定するところに
私たちの存在理由がある

私たちがそれを怠れば
いつか孫たちが問うだろう
「あなたたちの世代は何をしたのですか」と

一九八四年七月二三日、原発公判・福島地裁判決の日に

吉田　真琴（よしだ　まこと）
1933年〜1987年、福島県生れ。詩集『二重風景』。福島県いわき市に暮した。

文明の幻国

――ヒロシマからフクシマへ――

仁科　龍（にしな　りゅう）
1940年、新潟県生れ。『親鸞の妻・恵信尼』『歎異抄入門』、詩集『くもりガラスの時』。東京都板橋区に暮す。

濁流にのみこまれ
愚かな国策と知りながら
ロゴスなき闇を選んだこの国びと
重装備した兵士の上陸に
竹ヤリでたちむかう道しか知らず
原爆の投下をまねき
息の根止められて　めざめた焼野原
ヒロシマ・ナガサキの暗黒を背負って
歩いてきたのではなかったか　この国は

安全神話が創生されて
原発ひしめく　たかが島国
渦巻く欲望が幻視した繁栄の錦絵
世界の頂点にのぼりつめた気のこの国びとは
歴史の実像を知りながら　顔そむけ
新たな幻想の小道を　肩いからせて
ただ歩いてきただけではないのか
傲慢と幼稚のバーチャルに舞いあがり
自身の国の内部から
放射能を噴出しはじめている

致命的な崩壊が始まっているのではないのか
でも　かつての大本営発表をなぞるように
事がらの真実はどこからも語られない
フクシマ原発　メルトダウン
気層の裂け目を吹き荒れる熱風のうねり
むき出しの肌を灼いてくる陽ざしの中で
ただ　立ちつくす

風にも光にも放射能が乱舞しているのに
誰も見ることなく　なすすべもなく
生と死の時の流れに　落在している

何をしたらよいですか？

紺碧の空に光る
瑠璃色のモスク
アリババと四十人の盗賊たちの
不思議な話を夢のなかで聞いた
――少年時代――
バグダッドの市場では
盗まれたアラジンの魔法のランプが
いまも灯されているか

大学小児科のジョルマクリ先生は言う
　病院の廊下にさえあふれる白血病の子供たち
　処方する薬を持たない医者に何ができますか？
ヒロシマの医者は、五十八年前、
　患者さんに何をしましたか？
答えることのできない質問に
僕の記憶中枢はあの日の閃光に灼かれ
僕は黙って下を向く

若い母親の腕に抱かれた
白血病の子供たちの無心な笑顔

御庄　博実（みしょう　ひろみ）
1925年、山口県生れ。詩集『御庄博実詩集』『原郷』『ふるさと―岩国』。
詩誌「火皿」、日本現代詩人会所属。広島県広島市に暮す。

まぶたごと目玉の飛び出した無脳児、水頭症………
机上に広がる異形の写真
凝視しながら　僕は盲目となる

バスラからやってきたアル‐アリ先生は言う
　処方する薬を持たない医者に
　何ができる？
　何をしましたか？
　何をしたらよいと思いますか？
　ヒロシマの医者の答えが聞きたいのです

机いっぱいに広がっている子供たち
耳元で囁きつづけるのは
お母さん　あなたですか
痩せ細った頰
真珠の瞳
やわらかい肌に
僕はそっと掌をあてる
冷たい！
氷の肌に

アインシュタインの声

サオーダケー
サオーダケー

真夏の昼過ぎ
寝ころんで新聞を読んでいると
不思議な抑揚をつけ
物干竿を売る男の声が聞こえてくる

八月六日
テニアン時間午前九時十五分十七秒
ヒロシマに原子爆弾（リトルボーイ）投下
このニュースが
マンハッタン計画（プロジェクト）を生んだ
アインシュタインに届いた時
彼は一言うめいただけであるという

Oh, weh !

そして
死ぬ
五か月前の遺言のような言葉

小松　弘愛（こまつ　ひろよし）
1934年、高知県生れ。詩集『狂泉物語』『どこか偽者めいた』『のうがええ電車　続・土佐方言の語彙をめぐって』。詩誌「兆」。高知県高知市に暮す。

――今度生れ変ったら、科学者や教師にはならないで、
ブリキ職人か行商人になりたい。

サオーダケー
サオーダケー
サオーダケー

竿竹を買う人はだれもいないようだ
窓の外に
空はヒロシマのように晴れわたっている

Oh, weh !

町角を曲がったのだろうか
行商人アインシュタインの声が
しだいに遠ざかってゆく

＊weh［ve: ヴェー］…ドイツ語・（苦痛・悲嘆などの気持ちを表して）ああ、おお。

トマトのように

フライパンを火にかけ　油をひいて
ミニトマトを入れた
プチッと薄い皮だけむけた

赤い肉がむきだしになる
油がじわっと浸(し)みていく
ソースもじんわり染(し)みていく
痛そうだ

皮がむけてたれさがった
被爆者(ひばくしゃ)の赤い肉
リンパ液がしみだす　のどがかわく

あの日　人間がトマトのように焼かれた
焼かれたトマトは白い足で
逃げまどった

悪魔のおもちゃ　で

川奈　静（かわな　しずか）
1936年、千葉県生れ。詩集『ひもの屋さんの空』『花のごはん』。日本詩人クラブ所属。千葉県南房総市に暮す。

神話の推移

谷崎　眞澄（たにざき　ますみ）
１９３４年、北海道生れ。詩集『谷崎眞澄詩選集一五〇篇』『喪失』『夜間飛行』。
詩誌「極光」「パンと薔薇」、小樽詩話会所属。北海道札幌市に暮す。

チェルノブイリを知っている者も
チェルノブイリを知らない者も
赤ん坊　幼児　少年少女たちの
卵のように神秘的で　デリケートな
内部のやわらかな内臓　骨などの敏感な感受性を
いまは確かなこととして知っているだろう

海岸線に沿って　十数機も繋がる原発が
どんな意味を持つのか　深い考えもなく
建ててしまい　恐れることがなかった

「死んだ者はいません」
「べつだん異常はありません」
すでに　われわれは知っていた
太平洋の核実験の惨状
セミパラチンスクの狂気
劣化ウラン弾を打ち込まれたイラクの子供たち

たとえば甲状腺癌の痛々しさは
チェルノブイリの子供たちの
首筋の傷痕が物語っている

住んでいた者も　住んでいなかった者も
確かめねばならない
「住んでいた場所」は
帰る条件が整ったか

生まれたところに帰ることができるのは
神話かもしれないなんて！

　がれきにひそむものまでみていなければならない
たわわに実った果実の言葉と沈黙を
聞き分けなければならない

ヘレン・ケラーのゆびさき

「周りのひとは何もいわず
　わたしに顔を触らせてくれました」

昭和二十三年に再来日を果たし
広島を訪れたヘレン・ケラーは
被爆者のケロイドに直に触れ
原爆の悲惨さを理解した

視覚も聴覚も失ったヘレンにとって
触れることが世界を知る唯一の術(すべ)であった
そしてヘレンの細いゆびさきは
健常者の目や耳の感覚を超えて
人類の不条理をあまねく読み取った

もしもヘレンがいま福島を訪れ
ゆびさきで大地をなぞったとすれば
どのような叫びがその虎膚を突き抜け
ヘレンの魂を揺さぶることだろう

目はあっても何も見ることができず
耳はあっても何も聞くことのできない
束の間の繁栄に執着するだけの
わたしたちの罪を受け止めるように
ヘレンのゆびさきは不条理と対峙する

ああわたしも血の通ったゆびさきで
愛(いつく)しむように大地をなぞりたい
そして目を見開き耳を澄まし
未来へのバトンをこの手で渡したい

志田　昌教（しだ　まさのり）
1953年、長崎県生れ。詩人会議、福岡詩人会議、スイング所属。長崎県佐世保市に暮す。

全てをかえせ

秋山　泰則（あきやま　やすのり）
1938年、東京都生れ。詩集『流砂』『民衆の記憶』『泣き坂』。日本ペンクラブ、日本現代詩人会、松本詩人会所属。長野県松本市に暮す。

無人となった集落で
牧舎に繋がれた牛が
木柵に歯形を深く残して
幾十頭となく倒れて死んだ

その干からびた体毛から
空を蹴っているひずめから
牧舎の錆びた鉄の柱から
床の土から
屋根裏の窪みから
草の根　木の幹　大気から
ひそかに窺がっているものがある

体に染み入ってくる死の衝撃は
永遠の第一歩を踏み出した
広島　長崎の地表を覆うコンクリートを押し上げ
ビキニ環礁の海底から立ち上がり
第五福竜丸を漂流させ
少数を圧死させる

我慢をしてはならない
我慢をすることは逃げていることだ
耐えることは真実を視ないのと同じことだ
痛いときは大声で痛いといい
痛い痛いといいながら
痛みの元を探さなくてはならない

放射線をばら撒かれ故郷を追われた人たちを
少数のままにしてはならない
待たせてはならない
見たくないものは見えないものとし
あってはならないことは
はじめから存在しないものとしてきた人たちに
声をそろえていわなくてはならない
牛をかえせ　牛の餌をかえせ
家をかえせ畑をかえせ草をかえせ木をかえせ
水をかえせ空気をかえせ虫も魚も鳥もかえせ
隣の人たちをかえせ
これから生まれてくる子どもたちの平和をかえせ
其処にあったものは全てかえせ
其処から生まれる未来をかえせ

フクシマ

二〇一一年三月十一日　午後二時四十六分
東北地方太平洋沖地震発生
マグニチュード　九・〇

東京電力　福島第一原子力発電所
　原子炉緊急停止
同午後三時二十七分
津波　第一波襲来
推定十五メートル

一号機
三月十一日　午後三時三十七分
　全交流電源喪失
ＥＣＣＳ（非常用炉心冷却システム）停止
同午後五時
　燃料露出
同午後八時
――メルトダウン
三月十二日　午後三時三十六分
水素爆発

本多　照幸（ほんだ　てるゆき）
１９５３年〜２０１４年、埼玉県生れ。『*JAREBONG*』（共著）『*Global Marine Radio-activity Database*』。詩誌「炎樹」。千葉県市川市に暮らした。

同午後七時四分
　海水注入

二号機
三月十一日　午後三時四十一分
　全交流電源喪失
三月十三日　午後一時二十五分
　ＥＣＣＳ停止
同午後四時三十四分
　海水注入
同午後六時
　燃料露出
同午後十一時
――メルトダウン
三月十五日　午前六時十分
水素爆発
　圧力抑制室破損

三号機
三月十一日　午後三時三十八分

　全交流電源喪失
三月十二日　午前十一時三十六分
　ＥＣＣＳ停止
三月十三日　午前八時
　燃料露出
三月十四日　午前十一時
水素爆発
同午後十時
――メルトダウン

放出放射能量
大気中
　七十七万兆ベクレル
海水中
　四七二〇兆一五〇〇億ベクレル
国際原子力事象評価尺度
――レベル七（最高）
避難区域外へ避難した人
　十二万人超
ＩＡＥＡは言う
――安全神話あって
　　安全文化なし

今も
十二万トン
七十二万兆ベクレル
を孕んだ
高濃度汚染水が滞留
毎日五〇〇トン増え続け
建屋ばかりか
心臓に穴の開いた
原子炉は
水棺さえままならず
いつまで待ったら
石棺は
できるのか
いつになったら
成仏できるのか
いつになったら

（二〇一一年六月三十日）

職歴が止まった日

原　発子（はら　はつこ）
1941年、山梨県生れ。埼玉県川越市に暮す。

二〇一一年八月三十一日
私の職歴が止まった
会社を辞めたのだ

三・一一以降　突然
私の机の上が書類の山になった
夜十時　十一時まで働いた
土、日もなく会社へ行った
月曜日、出社すると机はまた書類の山
毎日が書類の山との格闘
これもみんなに電気を届けるため
夫の姿は眼中から消え
二人の子供は舅姑まかせ
これが私の真骨頂と
体が動かなくなるまで働いて働いて

七月
私のからだが赤信号を発した
朝　会社に入ると動悸がした
書類の山の前に座ると眩暈がした
手が震えて字が書けなくなった
字がかすんで読めなくなった
昼食が近づくと嘔気がした
電車の駅を降り違えた
これは何かの間違いだと思った
私の心が甘えているのだと思った
原発の派遣労働者のことを考えた
がんばらなければと思った
我慢してがまんして働き抜こうと思った

誰にも話さなかった
入社時に私が両親に言った言葉を
「お父さん　お母さん
原発反対運動をやらないで下さい
私も東京電力の社員のひとりですから」

誰にも言えなかった
その時　母から返ってきた言葉を
「それはあなたの人生です
親には親の人生があります

良いことは誰がやっても良いことですが
ダメなことは誰がやってもダメです
人間のやることに完全にありません
原発は原爆と同じですから」

あの頃は就職氷河期だった
先生に手紙を書いたら返事がきた
「すぐ面接にいらっしゃい」と
うれしかった
自分の力で就職できることがうれしかった
経済と環境の関係を説いた先生
私は先生の人格を信じた
面接場所は東京電力株式会社

仕事は楽しかった
灯りを作り出す会社の仕事に誇りを感じた
結婚相手も見つけて
子供もふたり産んだ
同期の女の子は　みんな退職した
残ったのは天下りのおじさんたちだけ

私の仕事？
福島原子力発電所の労務管理

と言っても　派遣労働者は管理外
放射能モレ事故があっても
それは派遣労働者の仕事
危険な仕事は派遣持ちだから
週二日以上は働けない派遣労働者
いつも放射能に曝されているから
退職したら職歴を消される派遣労働者
病気の時の証明書に使われると困るから
派遣労働者の命は
東京電力の命ではないから

私は今
節電に腐心する一市民になった
原発の力を借りずに生きるために

チャーチロック&フクシマ

石川　逸子（いしかわ　いつこ）
1933年、東京都生れ。詩集『千鳥ヶ淵へ行きましたか』『ヒロシマ連祷』『ロンゲラップの海』。詩誌「兆」「詩区かつしか」。東京都葛飾区に暮す。

1

あのかすかな鳴き声は
地中に生きたまま　埋められた
チャーチロックの
山羊　牛　それとも　馬？

べとべとのベントナイトにからまれ
前足の先を僅かに地上に残して
地中に固められてしまった
ファニーおばさんの　山羊よ

白人の男たちは
ふいにやってきて　木を引き抜き
ダイナマイトで　あちこち穴を開け
用がすむとベントナイトを流しこみ
ファニーおばさんの抗議に
社長は陽が上がってくるほうに住んでいる
そっちへ言ってくれ　と答えた

男たちはウランを掘るのだ
ウラン鉱滓（こうさい）は　これから何万年　放射能を持ち続け
ナヴァホ族を肺がんにしていくだろう

ボタ山で遊んでいた
ファニーおばさんの九つの孫も
呼吸ができなくなって　夜中に死んだ

チャーチロックの深夜は
地中の動物たちの　はげしいすすり泣きで
驟雨（しゅうう）のようだ

死んだ坊やの泣き声は　混じっていないか
白髪のファニーおばさんは　暗いベッドに
起き上がり
じいっと　耳を澄ましています

2

かたときも　あなたが放さない
黒いビニール袋一つ
　（そのなかで泣いている　故郷
　　怒っている　故郷）

ツナミが来るようっ　だれかれの叫びに
夢中で高台へ　さらに高台へ
ツナミが引けば帰るつもりだったのに
フクシマ原発メルトダウン
着の身着のまま　避難所を転々
　（そのまま帰れなくなった　故郷）

一時帰宅は四ヶ月後　案じていたわが家は
流されず壊れもしないまま　荒れ果て
庭の山桜　栗の木　茄子　葱　茗荷
なつかしい里山　小川の岸辺も
見えない放射能に汚され
　（茫然と立ち尽くした　故郷）

防塵マスク　防水着　白い手袋　と
ものものしい姿で
わずかな時間　黒いビニール袋一つに
あせりながら詰めこんだ　あれこれ
アルバム　針箱は断念　位牌は入れて
　（無念のうちに離れるしかなかった　故郷）

数々の民話にはぐくまれて　生まれ育ち
七十八年間　あなたの　笑いと涙を
　（常に　見守り　励ましてくれた　故郷）

幾つめかの避難所で暮らす　あなたが　いま
かたときも放さない　怒りの　黒いビニール袋
離れ離れとなった　なつかしい友に呼びかけ
（原子村）めがけ　高く掲げる　黒いビニール袋

里山汚染

酒井　力（さかい　つとむ）
１９４６年、長野県生れ。詩集『水の天体』『虚無の空域』『白い記憶』。佐久文学火映、日本ペンクラブ、日本詩人クラブ所属。長野県佐久市に暮す。

春は山菜
秋には茸を採る
すぐ近くの山まで
それはやってきた

見えない
聴こえない
物音ひとつたてない

ふいに飛来し
この地に降りそそいだものは
やがて浸潤し
動物たちの足元に潜む
不透明な死への予兆になった

山は嘆いている
言葉にならない怒りを
木々の葉にさざめかせ
地下に落ちる
水琴の音に沈め

里山は荒れるだろう
手入れも危うく
山人も踏み込めない
今となれば

何一つ告げないまま
里山は
未来の頁に刻印するのだ
思い上がった
人間たちに向けて

おまえたちは
いったい
何をしてきたのだ
と

＊福島第一原発の爆発事故により、二〇一一年十一月、佐久市の山で基準値を超える放射線量が計測された。

飼い犬が見つめていた

木島　章（きじま　あきら）
1962年、神奈川県生れ。詩誌「エガリテ」、詩人会議所属。神奈川県横浜市に暮す。

鳶色の潤んだ瞳にうつる
フクシマの大地
人はそこに不毛を見るけれど。
野に放たれた家畜たちは
死の灰を巻き上げ悠然と駆けめぐる。

十年、それとも百年
原野は人を拒み続け。

テレビカメラを遠巻きに
画面から消えた犬たち
服従の遺伝子を放射線に断ち切られ
忘れたはずのオオカミの血を覚醒させるのか。

千年、いな万年
止められない細胞分裂。

動物たちは
放射能といっしょに
どんな進化をたどり

どんな世界を生きていくだろう
そのとき人間の居場所はあるのか。
牛や豚や馬を従えた犬たちは
廃炉になった建屋の頂きで
いっせいに雄叫びをあげる。

そんな夢にうなされて目を覚ますと
飼い犬が見つめていた
遠い未来から聞こえる仲間の声に
じっと耳を澄ましていたのか。
その潤んだ瞳にうつった私は
途方に暮れているだけだった。

「生きものの記録」異聞

三井　庄二（みつい　しょうじ）

1944年、山形県生れ。評論集『戦後映画論』『人間主義の文学教育』。詩誌「いのちの籠」。千葉県八千代市に暮す。

線量計が振り切れることもある
福島第一事故原発二〇キロ圏内
着のみ着のまま逃れた人間たち
ペットは野良猫や野良犬となる
牛舎や豚舎が閉じられたまま
飢え死にした家畜たち
ウジがわき皮と骨だけになった
生き残ったところで殺処分となる
野垂れ死にを免れた動物たちの
ワイルドライフ（放射線下の自由）
家畜でなくなった牛に子が生まれ
イノブタの家族が縦横に荒し回る

事故原発から六キロのところ
少ない餌で飼われても元気な
地域おこしのダチョウたち
わずかな燃料で大きな電力を生む
原発のシンボルというわけだ
バッグやベルトになる皮
クッキーやケーキになる卵

エキゾチックミートになる肉
観光資源にして畜産動物となった
寒冷と高湿度に弱いというのに
原発平和利用のマスコットである
三十羽のうち残ったボスと数羽
警戒区域は祖先の地アフリカだと
血が騒いで存分に疾駆していた
一年近く生きて危険動物とされ
捕獲作戦に六羽が捕まった　結局
研究対象（放射線影響）の動物に

ゴーストタウンに虚しく踊る標語
「原子力正しい理解で豊かなくらし」
「原子力郷土の発展豊かな未来」
人影の全くない町に残る店の看板
毎日新鮮回転寿司「アトム」
パチンコ・パーラー「ＡＴＯＭ」
送電の会社名「原子力運送」
原発の生贄に供された動物たちは
人間の今と子どもらの未来の姿だ

原発見学会

ゆきなか　すみお

1938年、京都府生れ。『ねこまたぎ2001』『ねこまたぎ2011』。詩誌「いのちの籠」。奈良県天理市に暮す。

真珠浜。美しい海の向こうに目指す原発が見えた。
白い円筒形の建物から
真っ白い雲のような水蒸気が吹きだしていた。
車は小さな湾を回って原発に近づいていく。
建物下の排水口から
コーヒーのような水が一面に泡を浮かべて勢いよく流れ
出ていた。

広報主任さんはしゃべり慣れた様子で原発の仕組みを説
明して、CO2を出さない地球にやさしいエネルギー、
安心で安全で、を強調されていた。

質問―白い水蒸気が出てましたけど放射能は漏れたりし
　てませんか？
広報―全く出ていないことはありませんが、ただちに人
　体に影響はありません。
質問―排水口の水は真っ茶色でしたけど大丈夫ですか？
広報―原子炉を冷やしただけの水ですから、ただちに人
　体に影響はありません。
主任さんは笑みをうかべて明確で明快だ。

時間間際に僕は手をあげた。
質問―この浜の魚、主任さんは家で食べてはりますか？
広報―いいえ。私の家では食べません。
質問―きれいな海ですけど、子供さんをここで泳がして
　はりますか？
広報―いいえ。子供はこの海では泳がせません。
ここでも広報さんは明確で明快だ。

見学会からもう二十年以上になる。
原発銀座と呼ばれる若狭の海と若狭の魚。
いまもときどき思いだす。

１００万年の詐取

藤谷　恵一郎（ふじたに　けいいちろう）
１９４７年、愛媛県生れ。詩集『風の船』『喪失の宙』『風を孕まず　風となり』。
関西詩人協会、日本詩人クラブ所属。大阪府豊中市に暮す。

すこやかな指が
夢みる掌が

青空をつかむように
永遠にタッチしそうに

たんぽぽやれんげ草の
広がる草はらに――

＊

だが　私たちは
そんな日常に癒されながら

永遠の木陰から
はみ出そうとしていた
あるいは追い出されようとしていた

太陽の遺伝子を
惑星に移植する者よ！

バベルの塔から
太陽に弓する者よ！

己の数十年の繁栄に
安全神話で
日本列島
１００万年の時を詐取することに
なるのではないか

千年に一度の想定外に対応できなかった
技術で　機構で　資本で　政治で
１００万年の地殻変動の想定外に
高レベル放射性廃棄物を晒すことに
なるのではないか

福島原発１号機の水素爆発の瞬間
――壁の漆喰が毀れ落ちるかのように
青空に浮かび　張り付いた
永遠の顔が　歪んで

消えるのを見たように思う

＊

祈りの風が
日本列島を
北から
西から
静かに吹いている

私たちの胸の中で

たんぽぽやれんげ草の広がる
放射性汚染の
言葉を持たぬ命の草はらで――

（『叢生』１７６号２０１１・10一部改）

千万ドルの夜景

目映さに憧れて
大都会は
あざやかな
渇く宝石

闇には
きらめく光が
似合いすぎていた

過疎地の
海岸に立ち並ぶ
巨大な湯沸しポット
ウランが茹でられて
発生する放射能
幾千万のイルミネーションの
豪華な楽園を支えている
やさしい泉のように
にこやかでありながら
秘かに毒になり
海に捨てられていた

奇形の魚が泳ぐ夜の海
水面の鏡にゆらゆら漂う
月の影は訊いている
嘘のない現象
海底からの淡い悲鳴
潮騒の予知夢の喘ぎ
卵を産んではならないと
怯えている

千万ドルの夜景は
泥酔した欲望をなぐさめて
はち切れるように美しい
星や月の光よりもきらめき
放射能を泡立てる
何も聴こえていない
無人になった記憶の在り処
溢れるほどの
人工の輝きだって
心から微笑んではいない

水月　りら（みづき　りら）
1963年、京都府生れ。詩集『にじのはし』。詩誌「PO」、現代京都詩話会、詩人会議所属。京都府舞鶴市に暮す。

あしたの歌を

杉本　知政（すぎもと　ともまさ）
1932年、岡山県生れ。詩集『迷い蝶』『風の声』『沈黙への質問』。詩誌「COAL SACK」「径」。岡山県赤磐市に暮す。

あの日二〇一一年三月十一日東日本大震災の中から
悪魔はいきなり姿を現わした
その日までこの星に生きる人々の多くは
原発を夢の灯と信じもてはやしてきた
永遠のしあわせをもたらす宝物と思い込み
虹を仰ぐように称えもしていた
けれどもそれは全く誤りであったことを
大震災は厳しく教えてくれていた
多くの犠牲者への深い悲しみと鎮魂の祈り
被災者の苦しみを慰撫する言葉の満ちる中
全く新たな苦悩を原発はもたらしたのだった
仮面をぬいだ怪物の真の姿と
そのまがまがしい振舞いの全貌を知る者は
この星に皆無であるといってもよかった
悪魔は次々と見えない魔の手をふるい
人々は見極められない事象にとまどい
迷い続けねばならなかった
これまで人類が持つ科学技術文明の知識と技の檻では
あの悪魔は制御できていなかったのである
不確かな檻への過信は潔く捨て去り
一刻も早い悪魔との訣別が求められている
いま私達が住んでいる星　地球
これからも友と手を重ね苦楽を共に分け合うところ
大きく眼を見開きまわりを見詰めてみよう
豊かな自然に満ち溢れているのが視えるから
真赤に燃える太陽の笑顔
蒼空と雲の思いを浮べる水　水　水
限りないいのちの声満ちる森の草木
高く低くうたうように囁くように漂う風の声
逞しく両手を広げ日々の糧を産む大地
たぎり立つ熱い想いを迸しらせるマグマの想い等々（などなど）
優しくふところに嬰児を抱きしめる母のように
地球はここに住む全部の生命を慈しんでいる
陽の光・水と風の手　樹木に潜む焔の色　大地の想い
その総ての力を合わせることが
必ず未来を照らす希望の光になる筈である
さあ歩み始めよう心を重ね知識の扉を開くために
そして祈り続けていよう
被災地へ一日も早く安らかな暮しの戻ることを
笑顔に満ちた明日を賛える歌の聞こえる日の来ることを

わが浪江町

根本　昌幸（ねもと　まさゆき）
1946年、福島県生れ。詩集『海へ行く道』『昆虫詩篇』『昆虫物語』。詩誌「ゆすりか」「PO」、日本詩人クラブ所属。福島県相馬市に暮す。

いつから福島がフクシマになったのか
うつくしまふくしまが
カタカナ文字のフクシマに。
福島県に私は生まれ育った。
それも双葉郡浪江町という所に。
海があり　山があり
二つの美しい川があり
みどりの豊かな町だった。
なぜ　そこを追われなければならないのか
答えてくれ
私は浪江町が好きだった。
誰よりも好きだった。
子どもの頃は魚つりをした。
鳥刺しをした。
山や川で遊んだ。
野原に寝ころんで
流れ行く雲を見た。
みんなみんな美しかった。
美しい心をしていた。
おとなになっても
純粋なままだった。
四季折々の花が咲き
人々は優しい気持ちをしていた。
わが浪江町。
この地に　いつの日にか
必ずや帰らなければならぬ。
地を這っても
帰らなければならぬ。
杖をついても
帰らなければならぬ。
わが郷里浪江町に。

故郷へ

大久保　せつ子（おおくぼ　せつこ）
１９４８年、福島県生れ。詩誌「炎樹」、詩人会議所属。東京都練馬区に暮す。

ふきのとう、うこぎ、たらの芽、わらび、せり
山にやわらかな芽吹きが
用意されるころ

田は起こされ　畑は耕され
牛舎で小牛が生まれ
馬は放牧され
鶏は卵を産み
命満ちる季節。

秋になれば
さわさわと揺れる稲穂
実りを告げる稲の匂い

長い長い時間をかけ
作られてきた土壌がもたらす
極上の恵み
受け継がれ守られてきた暮らし

潰えるのは一瞬だった。

人が制御できない原発の
破壊力ではない
目に見えない　無慈悲なもの
命を奪う放射能に
故郷は汚染された。

慈しみ世話をしてきた牛たちの殺処分
丹精こめて育ててきた競走馬を手放し
家や田畑や家畜を　捨て
追われるように逃げ
避難所を転々とする難民の暮らし

夢に見る
故郷の田畑、山々。

入り口を閉鎖された
故郷へ続く道よ、
春はまためぐり
荒れ果てた土地に
ふきのとう、うこぎ、たらの芽、わらび、せり
摘まれる日を待ちわびている。

青の胎動

芳賀　章内（はが　しょうない）
1933年、福島県生れ。詩集『せらみっくの都市』『直線の都市　円いけもの』、詩論集『詩的言語の現在』。詩誌「いのちの籠」。埼玉県さいたま市に暮す。

青い空の
青い声が
妊婦には聞こえている
未生の窓を破って
ただひとつの窓を破って
あり得べき玉の
ただひとつの位置を
探している

青は天にあり
海にある
青の氾濫を沈める
抑制を抱いて
妊婦は
いのちの海溝を泳ぎ
八〇〇〇メートルの深みに沈む
潮の流れを
体内深く確かめる
いつも　出発は
青であるように
深く

乗物のなかで
胎児は目醒める
つぎつぎと
胎児のなかで
胎児が目醒め
妊婦はそのたびに
重い手袋に
胎児を詰めて
空をみつめる

青い空の
青い声を
息吹きの地図に落とすとき
青の呪文が
地から湧きあがる
天の青は
祈りの化粧を手袋にほどこす
地の青は
寄せては返して
時を抜け出している

除染

鈴木　洋（すずき　ひろし）
１９５８年、福島県生れ。詩集『常少女』『僕の心の片隅の』。詩誌「詩脈」、福島県現代詩人会所属。福島県会津若松市に暮す。

わずか百数十年前
若き志士たちが血を流し
命を懸けて夢見た未来がここなのか

洗い流しても、削り取っても
故郷に帰れる日は遠い
故郷に帰れない悲しみは
誰が洗い流してくれるのだろう

本当に汚れているのは何処なのか
除染すべきは何なのか
武士（もののふ）たちの嘆きの声が聞こえる

まやかしだらけの世の中に
凛として立ち向かう勇気
真の除染はそこからしか始まらない

薄めてしまえ
汚れているとわからなくなるくらいに
洗い流してしまえ
見せかけだけの安心を取り戻せればそれでいい

表土を削り屋根や壁を洗う
除染という名のまやかし
２万年もの時を待たなければ
きれいにならないものを
どこに流すというのだ

福島の悲しみや怒りなど他人事
政治家は篤き志を忘れ去り
耳を疑うような発言ばかりを繰り返す
大臣を退いてもなお政治家は辞めず
党利、私欲に明け暮れる

原子力発電所が
放射性物質を拡散する大事故を起しても
誰も責任を取らない

いのちこそたから

太田　隆夫（おおた　たかお）
1937年、福島県生れ。詩集『風は記憶へと』『童戯考』『水影についての覚書』。詩誌「卓」、福島県現代詩人会、日本現代詩人会所属。福島県福島市に暮す。

もちろん　この前までは我が国特有のリアス式海岸と豊
　穣な海だった
山々は緑ふかく　山毛欅（ぶな）や櫟（くぬぎ）、ミズナラ　そして松の木
　栗の木が茂り
ひとびとは　平穏な暮しの日常を聡明に紡いできた
戦争が終り　渇望の平和をとり戻して　共感の力を灯し
　てきた
三陸沿岸から　いわき　茨城の五百キロもの海岸の
共感の六十余年の歳月は　マグニチュード九・〇に崩れ
　壊されて　流された

かつてわたし達は　広島　長崎　第五福竜丸の原爆と放
　射能被曝から
「核」の恐怖は　得体の知れないものと拒否しながら
「平和利用」という魔術に幻惑され
処世のなかで容認してしまってきた

そして政治と企業体の見事な連携は　福島という朗らか
　な地名を利用して
原子力発電所を建てつづけてきたのだった
突然の人津波は
虚構だった「安全神話」の四基もの建屋を一蹴し
水素爆発をおこして　放射性物質を撒き散らしている現
　実の悔しさ

ひとびとは　すべてを失うために生きてきたのではない
朝はひろがる光のなか　夜は星をめぐる言葉を交わし
濃密な魂の表現を　「いのちこそたから」として
胸に刻んで　生きてきたのだ

高村智恵子が「阿多多羅山の上にある空がほんとの空*」
　と言ったが
いま　こんなにも広く猪苗代湖を抱える
朗らかな「福島県」という土地は
無色無臭な放射性物質のため
年寄りから　いたいけな幼児の呼吸まで汚されている

避難できない子どもたちは運動会もなく
プールで飛沫もとばせない夏となってしまっている
向日葵畑の向う　蟬の鳴く林へも行けない寂しい切なさ

＊＝高村光太郎詩集『智恵子抄』の「あどけない話」より

（初出・『12クレマチス詩集』所収）

桃源境

木戸　多美子（きど　たみこ）
1959年、福島県生れ。福島県現代詩人会所属。福島県二本松市に暮す。

私の生まれた大地はもうない
緑の風がなびく彼方
太陽を十万年分詰めた菜の花が
静かに広がる場所だ
頬に触れる風は心地よい

私の生まれた海はもうない
磯の匂いに満ちた光り輝く波
銀色の魚が飛び跳ねる
ゆうゆうとした深い場所だ
足の爪に細かい砂が触れる
今もそこにあるのに

春の日から
どこもかしこも夢の続き
海も空も色を変えた
ぐれんの色
未来をいっとき止める色
塗り絵のように拡がり続け
夢の中の取り残された人々に発令される色
この悲しみは
悲しみが追いつかないほどの悲しみ

英雄も救世主も一時限り
ただオロオロするひとりの人間が
そこここにいるだけ
真空の闇に浮かぶ
青い球体の上での出来事
すべてはこれだけ
誰のせいにもしたくない
何かのせいにもしない
自然のせいにさえも

私の生まれた大地はもうない
私の生まれた海はもうない
緑の風がなびく彼方
磯の匂いに満ちた光り輝く波
もうここにはない
ないのだが
そこにある
そこに私は帰る
明日帰る
きっと帰る
私の生まれた大地
私の生まれた海

魂が駈ける場所

うおずみ　千尋（うおずみ　ちひろ）
１９４４年、福島県生れ。詩集『淩霄花』『憶』『牡丹雪幻想』。詩誌「衣」「COAL　SACK」、日本現代詩人会所属。石川県金沢市に暮す。

広い広い空でした
碧い碧い海でした
真っ白な砂丘が続いて深緑の松林が繁る
わたしが生まれ育ったところ
静かな海沿いの町
魂が駈ける場所でした

あの日
超えたものの叫びでしょうか悲鳴でしょうか
自然界の凄まじい変動
威力の前に
脆くも崩壊破綻した
人間が造り出して
人間に制禦出来ない
原子力

広島
長崎の
焼け爛れた記憶ずっしりと背負い
「No more」

祷りながら希いながら六五年歩いて来た
日本列島であったのに
道は
福島　あの海で途絶え
無惨に炸裂したのです

幻想も神話も一瞬に吹き飛ばし
終息不能物質は
音も無く形も無く影も無く
今日に降り積もり
明日へと流れ込みました
これが夢？
これが平和？

広い広い空でした
碧い碧い海でした
ふるさと　その町は
今も
わたしの
魂が還るところです

洗う

木塚　康成（きづか　やすなり）
1954年、広島県生れ。詩誌「火皿」。広島県呉市に暮す。

ランドセルに
名前を書き込んでも
背負う子供はもういません
泥の中からやっと見つけ出した野球帽は
誇らしげに破れていました
針も糸もなくて　おかあさんは
「ごめんね」とつぶやきながら
冷たい川の水で
手を真っ赤にして帽子を洗いました

泥の中には
果たされなかったたくさんの約束が埋もれています
あの日食卓に並ぶはずだった食器
期限が残された定期券
まっさらの学生服
未完のものはまだ他にもあります
知らない家族のアルバムです
最後にそれを閉じた人たちは
どこかで無事に寄り添っていると思うのです
そして
もっともっと温かい家族写真を
ここにもう一枚加えてほしい
泥まみれの写真は
知らない人たちに洗われて輝きだすのです

あの日　海は見たことがないほど凶暴でした
樹のなくなった褐色の大地に
悲しみの足跡は増え続け
放たれて群れをなした犬たちの咆哮が
日ごとに大きくなってゆきます
今　雨交じりの風が穏やかな海から
やさしく吹いています
ぼくたちの泥で汚れた額を洗い流すかのように
そう　水は何も悪いことをしていません
黒い水が膨らむのを止めないのはぼくたちのせいです
雨脚は激しくなるばかりです

うつくしい未来

未来の
うつくしい子供たちのために
今
わたしたちは手放さなければならぬ
永遠に消えない
「核」の火を。
それよりほかに
わたしたちに何ができるだろう
人の住めなくなった故郷を前にして

未来の
地球の子供たちのために
今
わたしたちは誓わなければならぬ
「フクシマ」の痛みを最後にすると。
この地上に
もう二度と
失なわれつづける故郷を作らないと。
心あるこの国の民よ
かつて
すべての生きとし生けるもののなかに仏性を見た
日本の民が尊んだ山川草木を
黒い雨で汚さないと。

何度でも
わたしは祈ることだろう
未来の渚で
子供たちが
遠い海から流れつく
色とりどりの貝殻を拾い集められるようにと。
今よりも　もっと
うつくしい未来が
百年先　ここに
訪れていますようにと。

浅山　泰美（あさやま　ひろみ）
1954年、京都府生れ。エッセイ集『京都　銀月アパートの桜』『京都　桜の縁し』、詩集『月暈』。詩誌「庭園」「孔雀船」、日本文藝家協会所属。京都府京都市に暮す。

鼓動

まだ間に合うと言う人がいる
もう手遅れだと泣き崩れる人がいる
ただちに問題は無いとうそぶく人も
それぞれに立場はあろうが大切な事が一つ

何も言わずに目を覆うのなら
此処に在る意味すら消えるのだ

世界が崩れていく音が聞こえるか?
いのちが、ほどけていくその声が
聞こえているか?　届いているか?

あの日、終わりを迎えた全てへ
これから、死にゆく全てへ
明日を生きる子供たちへ
在るままに暮らしていくあらゆる世界へ
どんな顔を出来ると言うのか
どんな言い訳を並べられると言うのか
今日と明日の区別のつく我々は
答えを出す義務を持ち続ける

眠る砂礫の一部となる前に
この、鼓動の導く方角へ
悲嘆と絶望に満たされる前に
魂の呼ぶ道を
ただ歩けば良い

還るべき道は確かに
記されている

北原　亜稀人（きたはら　あきと）
1983年、東京都生れ。短編集『*world is beautiful*』、小説『*Glorious city*』。
詩誌「COAL　SACK」。東京都江戸川区に暮す。

新しい人たちに

中村　純（なかむら　じゅん）
1970年、東京都生れ。詩集『草の家』『海の家族』。日本現代詩人会、日本詩人クラブ、詩人会議所属。京都府京都市に暮す。

新しい人たちに

あなたたちに詫びなければならない
素足で歩ける大地
思い切り倒れこめる雪原
せせらぎに飛沫をあげて歩く浅瀬の川
木漏れ日にふり仰ぐ森
色とりどりの落ち葉のプール
大地のエネルギーを蓄えた安全な作物
それらすべてを奪ってしまったことを

あなたたちに詫びなければならない
私たち大人の無知と無自覚と愚昧の結果
薄汚れた札束と引き換えに失われた日々
きらびやかな電飾の嘘
オール電化の指一本で回す生活
セシウム四百九十ベクレルのおしゃれなランチ
美しく盛り付けられた遺伝子組み換えのディナー

あなたたちに詫びなければならない
あなたのいのちの遺伝子が傷つき
あなたの体からはセシウムが検出され
あなたの甲状腺が腫れたこと

私たちにできることは
真実を探し続けること　伝え続けること
闘い続けること　あなたたちを連れて逃げること
ひとつひとつの野菜や肉や魚を選び
私たち自身の手でくらしを紡ぎなおすこと

もう一度はじめから　やり直そう
海が汚れる前の　土が汚れる前の　あの日
一番最初の　あのときから
じんるいが　間違えたあのとき
原子力発電所が　私たち女の胎内　いのちの源まで
まっすぐに　直進を始めた　あのとき

花盛りの桜が欲しい

ああ、ここに花盛りの桜が一本欲しい
白く凍てついた
この雪原の真ん中に！

淡い香りをはなつ
満開の桜に心を奪われて
固く凍った氷は
虚勢を張るのも忘れ
ゆるゆると緩んで
解けていくだろうか。

かすかな風に散るはなびらが
少女の吐息のように
その面にかかると
白い仮面の雪原は顔をくれないに染め
つつしみを忘れて
ゆるゆると解けていくだろうか。

花盛りの桜が一本欲しい！
降りしきるうす紅の花びらが
私のかじかんだ心を解かすだろう。

放射能まじりの雪でもなく
まして原子の黒い雨でもなく
うす紅のはなびらを散らして
世界を暖める空。
裂かれた大地を癒すのは
うす紅のはなびらの雨。

天と地を結んで——

ああ、この白くつめたい雪原の真ん中に
一本の花盛りの桜が欲しい！

木村　淳子（きむら　じゅんこ）
1936年、北海道生れ。詩集『美しいもの』『ロッテ・クラマー詩選集』。詩誌「饗宴」、北海道詩人協会所属。北海道札幌市に暮す。

ほんとうは

真田　かずこ（さなだ　かずこ）
1952年、島根県生れ。詩集『新しい海』『奥琵琶湖の細波』。詩誌「山陰詩人」「トンビ」。滋賀県高島市に暮す。

いやなんです
ふるさとに帰れなくなるなんて

いやなんです
目に見えないものにおびやかされるのが

いやなんです
外で遊びたがる子を叱るなんて

いやなんです
線量計なんか首に下げているのは

いやなんです
同じ町の人々との絆が壊れてしまうのが

いやなんです
子どもたちの未来を奪ってしまうのが

いやなんです
秋になればやってくる水鳥たち
なにも知らず水草を食べてしまうのが

いやなんです
稚鮎の木の芽煮が作れなくなるのが

いやなんです
きれいな琵琶湖の景色が封印されてしまうのが

いやなんです
美しい国土が失われてゆくのが

いやなんです
原子力という怪物が

いやなんです

ステルス

壊れた街の
ひび割れて
歪んだ鏡のなかを
白服で通りすぎる
身体はぐずぐずに飛びまわり
顔は左右で食い違う

きれぎれの像は
ほとんど真っ直ぐ反射しない
つまりほとんど写らない
見えない
誰からも顔を探せないもの
それが
この世界へ投影されているわたしの
いまの姿

晴れ晴れと生きることは
もうない
皆を汚した大きな疑惑が横たわり
誰の応答もあやふや

焼き直しの昨日の喜びを探すばかり
誰が騙そうとしても
自分を騙そうとしても
もう分かっている
自分が汚したこの世界に
二度と正像では写らないこと
死が誰の背中にも
影を濃くしていること

大村　浩一（おおむら　こういち）
1961年、静岡県生れ。詩集『ファーゼライ』。詩誌「反射熱」、現代詩フォーラム所属。静岡県静岡市に暮す。

泊原発にて

日下　新介（くさか　しんすけ）
1929年、福井県生れ。詩集『ぼくらの緊急信号』『塩せんべいの唄』、詩撰集『核兵器廃絶の道』。詩人会議、北の詩人会議、北海道詩人協会所属。北海道札幌市に暮す。

道を行くと
原発にほど近い堀株(ホリカップ)海水浴場の
水着姿の子らの群れ

ぼくらはとまりん館*の見学を終えて
原発を見下ろす山の上に立つ
紺碧の日本海のほとり
科学の最先端をゆく泊原発の
異様な原子炉建屋と
行き場のない放射能廃液ドラム缶の貯蔵庫群

湾内　指呼(しこ)の間(かん)
岩内(いわない)の岸辺にも
波にたわむれる子どもたち

思い出しておくれ
この子らにとっては遠い歴史でさえある
ヒロシマとナガサキ
ビキニの海の水爆実験を

この海の18年前は
まだ記憶に生々しい奥尻島地震

そして　今年3月11日　東日本大震災
地震・津波の天変地異に
原発の炉心溶融(メルトダウン)

豊かな漁場
田畑や牧場の地下深く
地球の宿命ともいうべき地殻変動と
歴史の中で試されずみの
スリーマイル島やチェルノブイリ原発事故の忘却
幾百億の交付金とひきかえにふりまかれた「安全神話」

「原発を造ったのはみんなの責任です」
親への批判にこたえて訴えたのは東電社員の子ども
まき起こる論議をよそに政治判断の渦中にある日本の原発

夏の太陽(ひ)の照り返しをうけて輝く泊原発
いつの日
暴走する放射能に
子らの夢　消さないでおくれ！

＊「とまりん館」＝北電の原子力ＰＲセンター
＊「詩人会議」二〇一一年十月号の一部改稿

観念せい！

五十四基の原発に
すっぽり囲まれている日本列島は
まるで
囚われ人たちを隔離した
大海の刑務所のようである

そこの原子力村[*1]のジャングルの
魑魅魍魎は
原発マネーの「麻薬」で
「トロイの木馬」[*2]を仕立て
「安全神話」を発信してきた

二〇一一年三月一一日の
福島第一原発事故は水素爆発し
広島型原爆の１６８倍の放射能[*3]を撒き
原子炉の核燃料はメルトダウンした

原子力村の騙り屋たちは
それでも事故の全貌を隠しつづけ
「安全神話」の呪文を唱え

山口　賢（やまぐち　けん）
１９３２年、山口県生れ。詩集『山口賢詩集』『日々新しく』『未来人』。詩人会議、佐賀県詩人会議所属。佐賀県唐津市に暮す。

再稼働の「やらせ」を画策している

魂を売った者たちよ
国民は〝怒髪天を衝いているぞ！〟

一九四五年八月十五日の敗戦で
絶対主義的天皇制の「不敗神話」が
崩れた道を後追いする者たちよ

観念せい！

＊１＝原発マネーと原発利権の利益共同体
＊２＝内部に潜入して破壊工作を行う者
＊３＝セシウム１３７

原発増設の闇

大津波と　原発の闇よ
父母を返せ　子を返せ
人間と故郷を返せ
愛と笑い声を返せ

あぁ　福島原発事故死者を含め
逝った一万五千人を超える無念の人々
命からがら生き残った悲しみの人々
言葉も凍る　冷酷な深い闇よ
人間と生き物の慟哭と苦悩を見よ

安全という原発で生まれた
日本列島の桜の雄しべが花弁に変化し
花弁が裂けたり　五弁が四弁に変わる
奇形や　海のカメ・魚介の大量死
どうして　日本や世界の英知を
結集しようとしないのか？

広島・長崎での何十万人もの
酷い死と地獄をみた　実験済みの核を
再利用した恐るべき原発に
なぜ　いつまでもこだわるのか
またもや企む川内原発三号機の増設

小村　忍（こむら　しのぶ）
１９４３年、パラオ島生れ。紀行随筆『川内川物語』。鹿児島県詩人協会所属。
鹿児島県出水市に暮す。

甦るピアノ

壊れた音は
泥にまみれて　もがき　うめく
ピアノの脚　蓋　鍵盤は
あちこちに散らばり
埋まってしまった
解体の無念さ

無残な片鱗に
嘆く人の決意が
空の青に誓う

一つ一つに祈りをこめて
泥土の中から拾いあげる
パズルのように
修正していく

楽器店だった場所で
繰り広げられた
ピアノへの執着
だけではない
壊れた昔は　取り戻さねばならない

横田　英子（よこた　ひでこ）
1939年、大阪府生れ。詩集『風の器』『私の中を流れる川について』『川の構図』。詩誌「リヴィエール」「ガイア」。大阪府堺市に暮す。

多くの哀しみに
消えていった声にこたえよう

甦った
ピアノの旋律は
海鳴りを越える
水平線の彼方へも
風にのり
かもめの群れから
ちまたの人に伝える

紅花のはなばなの
オレンジの波間に
よろこびの協奏曲

ここが　深い泥土の中から
ピアノを掘り起こしたところ
ピアノに和して
晴れやかな声が聞こえる

（ある日のテレビニュースから）

波音　X

夢中で生きていると
時間が消える

しんどかったりつらかったりすると
時間の砂に足をとられる

佇んで波音ばかりが聴こえる時は
針が逆方向に動き出し
蜃気楼が追いかけてくる
ああしたかった
こうすればよかった

だが心臓に手を当ててみれば
いま生きているのだ

海辺に立って
陽光の空を見上げる

水金火木土に月と太陽
ここは太陽系第三惑星のはずだ

佐相　憲一（さそう　けんいち）

1968年、神奈川県生れ。詩集『心臓の星』『港』、詩論集『21世紀の詩想の港』。
詩誌「進化論」「COAL　SACK」、詩人会議所属。東京都新宿区に暮す。

昔の人のくらし
時計もなく毎日太陽や月を見て
風の声を聴き雨の声を聴き
海を見つめ土の上に立ち
食べるものを工夫し
住まいをつくり着るものをつくり
愛を交わしたか

いつの間にか戦が大きくなり
いつの間にか貧富の差が大きくなり
いつの間にか支配関係がはっきりして
いつの間にかハラキリとか
いつの間にか侵略戦争とか
いつの間にか世界大戦とか
いつの間にか東西冷戦とか
いつの間にか在日米軍基地とか
いつの間にかグローバリズム競争とか
いつの間にか歴史教科書改ざんとか
いつの間にか自衛隊海外派兵とか

いつの間にか原発銀座とか
いつの間にかコマーシャリズムとか
いつの間にか百円ショップの若者とか
いつの間にか二十一世紀
放射能と格差社会である

自分の体に触れてみる
手、足、胸、腹、尻、背中、顔、鼻、口、目、髪
この頃気になる体内も奥に確かに
胃腸、肝臓、膵臓、腎臓、心臓
脳、血管、骨
もっと気になる内側には
〈こころ〉の気配

万葉集の無名詩人の人体と
ユーラシア原始クロマニョン人の人体と
ほとんど同じ構造の
この体

こころは
進化しただろうか

あんなに人気だったデジタル時計はもうはやらない
シンプルな腕時計を見ると

針は確かに未来の方へ
ほら　太陽の周りをこの星も
動いている

今夜は月が見られるだろうか
明日また太陽は照らしてくれるだろうか

時間が無い無いと言いながら
夕焼けの海に立つと

〈時間はある
　やれることはある〉

生きるんだと

新しい波音が聴こえてくる

再起動

今日の平和は曇天
今日の貧しさは晴天
正義の堤防の内側で
いなくなった人の影が踊る
サンクチュアリには
花が咲く日も近いだろう
影は一人二人と増えてゆく
失われたものの値に
いつまでも頭を垂れて
泣いている人もいる
それもいい　仕方がない
と皆思う
春が来る　だから泣いてはいけない
と皆眠る
少しずつ季節が成長し
卵白のように危うく
夢は育つ

　何人の天使を見ましたか
　　天使だとなぜわかりましたか

　　　裏切っていないと確かめましたか

ひんやりとした分厚いコンクリートの壁を背に
医師は尋ね続ける

答えられない　答えられない

　天使を捜しましょう
　　僕も手伝います
　　　遺伝子組成に影響が出るのです

如月の箱に
卵子を詰めて
頑なに女は目を瞑る

＊「別冊・詩の発見」第十一号発表作品

渡辺　めぐみ（わたなべ　めぐみ）
1965年、東京都生れ。詩集『ベイ・アン』『光の果て』『内在地』。詩誌「ウルトラ」、日本現代詩人会、六本木詩人会所属。東京都世田谷区に暮す。

聴乎無声

下村　和子（しもむら　かずこ）
1932年、兵庫県生れ。詩集『いろはにほへど…』『手妻』、エッセー集『森を探しに』。日本文藝家協会、日本現代詩人会、日本詩人クラブ他所属。大阪府大阪市に暮す。

縄文杉が　七千年を生きられたのは
あの遠い山の　深い暗さの故だ
屋久島の山中は　夜は真の闇
人は歩くことも　視ることもできない
森の王者として樹は場を守る
私は二食分の弁当を持って早発ちし
黙々と十時間歩いて近付いた
一日は　太陽と共に始まり　日の入りで終る

未知の星の宇宙人が地球探索に来たとしても
夜は地球を見付けられなかっただろう
樹もまた　夜は眠る
暗さは樹にも生きものにも　豊かな眠りを与え
陽光は　神だった
神の光の中で　海も山も樹も人も
穏やかに　小さな幸せを守って暮らした

夜も昼も　ギラギラと眩しく明るくなった地球
太陽は　神の座を失い
大阪の街路樹は驚くほど短命と聞く

石油　そして原子力が　世界を支配する
宇宙のルールは破れ
人の作った文明の都合の良さに酔い
やがて　自らの作ったものに　脅える
理解できなくなった海は
方向を探りながら　吠え　のたうつ
本然のものは　それぞれに苦しみ　渦巻く

心の闇を照らす仏像も
ライトアップされた擬似灯明に迷い
明る過ぎる科学の灯の下で
仏性を失った　美術品として立っておられる
全てを許し　あるがままに――
仏の本質は　赦（ゆる）しであるのだから――

私たちが　気付くしかないのだ
聴くしかないのだ　地球の声を

地獄の火

原発基地の上を鳥が飛び回り
ひび割れた青空は不快な雲を浮かべ
のどかな海岸線に白波が戯れ
何も知らない生き物は暮らしを憩う
緑地の迷宮
突然空から鳥が落ちて死に
田圃に奇形の蛙が現われるのだが
気に留める者もいなかった
専門家ですらこのくらいの価は
何の心配もないですよと言うが
地域の住民は高い数値の
放射線を浴びていたのだ
妊婦と子供は影響を受けやすく
住み慣れた故郷を離れた
すると大きな水素爆発が地を轟かせると
川の水は苦よもぎ*に汚染され
多くの者はその水を飲んだ
肉体は高温に熱せられ生気を失い
破滅の道にと至らしめる

この時期に不気味な地獄の釜を

片桐　歩（かたぎり　あゆむ）
1947年、長野県生れ。詩集『不条理の森』『美ヶ原台地』。長野県詩人協会所属。長野県松本市に暮す。

稼動させて良いのだろうか
自動制御つきと言うのだが
これほど当てにならぬ絶対値はない
不完全な人間は操作ミスを冒すもので
小さな事故らしいものはたびたび
放射能も建物に漏れ出して
内部被曝もたまにはあった
取り扱う者は正確さを欠き安易だ
ひとたび点火した火は永久に燃える
「神の灯火」なのだ
青白い燐光の炎を消化することなど
人間の技では立ちいかない
燃えたウランは違う元素に分裂し
飛び散った死の灰は空気と混わり
地表の泥にたまり害*を及ぼす
眼に見えない悪魔の物質は
知らない内に臓器に取りつき破壊し
命の火を奪いにくる

＊ヨハネ黙示録八章十一節より引用

からっぽの地球

佐藤　文夫（さとう　ふみお）
１９３５年、東京都生れ。詩集『昨日と今日のブルース』『ブルースマーチ』『津田沼』。詩誌「炎樹」、詩人会議、日本現代詩人会所属。千葉県佐倉市に暮す。

地球はいま何者かに蹴り上げられて
宙たかく舞い上がり
銀河系の隅っこまで吹き飛ばされていく

この地球を待っている　ゴールとは何か
銀河系の一番奥で地球を待ってるものは何か
燃えさかる太陽の業火か　ブラックホールか

やがて地球は　巨大な隕石群の中に突入する
蹴り上げられなおも宙たかく舞い上がる地球
落ちては蹴られ蹴られては落ち　するうちに
地球の中身は　そっくり　こぼれ落ち……

中身はからっぽ　空洞の地球だけが
だだっ広い宇宙をふらふらとさまよっている
舞い上がっては落ち　落ちては舞い上がる

かつて　この星に棲息していたものたち
すべてが　ふるい落とされ　こぼれ落ち
そこにいまは　もう何もない　誰もいない

何もない　誰もいない地球だけが　いま
真っ暗なだだっ広い宇宙をさまよっている

芽吹き

福本　明美（ふくもと　あけみ）
１９４９年、高知県生れ。詩集『ぷるん』『月光（つきあかり）』。詩誌「ＯＮＬ」、中四国詩人会所属。高知県四万十市に暮す。

農作物に花が咲き　鶯が鳴き始める
山つつじが咲き　山桜が咲く
穏やかな春の風景に　風に運ばれて
見えない放射能の恐怖が落ちる

原発を反対した人々も
原発を推進した人々も
恐怖が骨の髄まで浸透しているあいだは
さん　テン　いち　いち　は
記号にはならない　風化はしない
原発の事故を伝えていく　この先数十年
放射性物質が自然界に溢れ出るまえに
天罰でないことを知ろう

虫が這い出てくる季節になったが
静かに病んで絶えているだろうか
ほとぼりが冷めるまで
環境に合わせて進化するだろうか
生きて暮らしていくために
畔から作り始める季節になっても
田の神をもてなすこともできない
残された動物　虫や蝶　鳥に
人間の情は伝わるだろうか

突然断ち切られ視線を地面に落した日から
人は身体を動かしている
少々の事では動じなくなった人々が
魂の安定を求めて　土地を大事にしていく
競い合う枝々に　落葉に放射能は蝕んでいく
事も　なおざりにはしない

しなる自然の下剋上は　赤子の手を潰すように
日本列島が　捻じれて大きくへこむ前に
原発を廃止しよう

胸の中の空気が緑に染まるよう
自然の恩恵にあやかろう
驕ることなく巡ってくる春は
現在から未来へと永遠に続くよう
ほとばしる血の流れで　祈りの深さで
三月の気温を忘れないでいよう

詩作品の出典

本書『福島からの反響音――日本の詩人50人の発信』（リア・ステンソン、猿川アロルディ麻緒 編、Inkwater Press、二〇一四年）を構成する詩編はもともと、二〇一二年にコールサック社より出版された『脱原発・自然エネルギー218人集』（鈴木比佐雄・若松丈太郎、矢口以文、鈴木文子、御庄博実、佐相憲一 編、郡山直、矢口以文、木村淳子、結城文、島田桂子、棚瀬江里哉、沢辺祐子 訳）に掲載された作品です。下記のリストは、本書に掲載の50編を『脱原発・自然エネルギー218人集』の掲載順に、章立てとページ番号にしたがって列記したものです。これらの詩作品の詳細およびコールサック社刊行の書籍については、コールサック社（〒173−0004 東京都板橋区板橋2−63−4−509、Eメール：suzuki@coal-sack.com）までお問い合わせください。